Douglas MacArthur

These and other titles are included in The Importance Of biography series:

Alexander the Great	Adolf Hitler
Muhammad Ali	Harry Houdini
Maya Angelou	Thomas Jefferson
Louis Armstrong	Mother Jones
James Baldwin	Chief Joseph
Clara Barton	John F. Kennedy
The Beatles	Martin Luther King Jr.
Napoleon Bonaparte	Joe Louis
Julius Caesar	Douglas MacArthur
Rachel Carson	Malcolm X
Charlie Chaplin	Thurgood Marshall
Charlemagne	Margaret Mead
Cesar Chavez	Golda Meir
Winston Churchill	Michelangelo
Cleopatra	Wolfgang Amadeus Mozart
Christopher Columbus	John Muir
Hernando Cortes	Sir Isaac Newton
Marie Curie	Richard M. Nixon
Charles Dickens	Georgia O'Keeffe
Emily Dickinson	Louis Pasteur
Amelia Earhart	Pablo Picasso
Thomas Edison	Elvis Presley
Albert Einstein	Jackie Robinson
Duke Ellington	Norman Rockwell
F. Scott Fitzgerald	Eleanor Roosevelt
Dian Fossey	Anwar Sadat
Anne Frank	Margaret Sanger
Benjamin Franklin	Oskar Schindler
Galileo Galilei	William Shakespeare
Emma Goldman	John Steinbeck
Jane Goodall	Tecumseh
Martha Graham	Jim Thorpe
Lorraine Hansberry	Mark Twain
Stephen Hawking	Queen Victoria
Ernest Hemingway	Pancho Villa
Jim Henson	H. G. Wells

Douglas MacArthur

by Mary Virginia Fox

Lucent Books, P.O. Box 289011, San Diego, CA 92198-9011

Library of Congress Cataloging-in-Publication Data

Fox, Mary Virginia.
    The importance of Douglas MacArthur / by Mary Virginia Fox.
      p.   cm. — (The importance of)
    Includes bibliographical references and index.
    Summary: Describes the childhood, training, career, and
contributions of the man known for his military leadership
during World War II.
    ISBN 1-56006-545-1 (lib. bdg. : alk. paper)
    1. MacArthur, Douglas, 1880–1964—Juvenile literature.
2. Generals—United States—Biography—Juvenile literature.
3. United States—Army—Biography—Juvenile literature.
4. United States—History, Military—20th century—Juvenile
literature.   [1. MacArthur, Douglas, 1880–1964. 2. Generals.]
I. Title. II. Series.
E745.M3F69   1999
355'.0092—dc21   98–49749
                                             CIP
                                             AC

Copyright 1999 by Lucent Books, Inc., P.O. Box 289011,
San Diego, California, 92198-9011

Printed in the U.S.A.

Contents

Foreword

THE IMPORTANCE OF biography series deals with individuals who have made a unique contribution to history. The editors of the series have deliberately chosen to cast a wide net and include people from all fields of endeavor. Individuals from politics, music, art, literature, philosophy, science, sports, and religion are all represented. In addition, the editors did not restrict the series to individuals whose accomplishments have helped change the course of history. Of necessity, this criterion would have eliminated many whose contribution was great, though limited. Charles Darwin, for example, was responsible for radically altering the scientific view of the natural history of the world. His achievements continue to impact the study of science today. Others, such as Chief Joseph of the Nez Percé, played a pivotal role in the history of their own people. While Joseph's influence does not extend much beyond the Nez Percé, his nonviolent resistance to white expansion and his continuing role in protecting his tribe and his homeland remain an inspiration to all.

These biographies are more than factual chronicles. Each volume attempts to emphasize an individual's contributions both in his or her own time and for posterity. For example, the voyages of Christopher Columbus opened the way to European colonization of the New World. Unquestionably, his encounter with the New World brought monumental changes to both Europe and the Americas in his day. Today, however, the broader impact of Columbus's voyages is being critically scrutinized. *Christopher Columbus,* as well as every biography in The Importance Of series, includes and evaluates the most recent scholarship available on each subject.

Each author includes a wide variety of primary and secondary source quotations to document and substantiate his or her work. All quotes are footnoted to show readers exactly how and where biographers derive their information, as well as provide stepping-stones to further research. These quotations enliven the text by giving readers eyewitness views of the life and times of each individual covered in The Importance Of series.

Finally, each volume is enhanced by photographs, bibliographies, chronologies, and comprehensive indexes. For both the casual reader and the student engaged in research, The Importance Of biographies will be a fascinating adventure into the lives of people who have helped shape humanity's past and present, and who will continue to shape its future.

IMPORTANT DATES IN THE LIFE OF DOUGLAS MACARTHUR

1880
Douglas MacArthur born in an army fort in Little Rock, Arkansas, on January 26.

1919
Becomes superintendent of West Point.

1914–1918
World War I; as head of the Rainbow Division, MacArthur is promoted to rank of general.

1929
Divorced from Louise MacArthur.

1903
MacArthur graduates from West Point and is commissioned a second lieutenant.

1880	1890	1900	1910	1920	1930

1887
MacArthur graduates from the West Texas Military Academy at Fort Sam Houston, Texas.

1903
First tour of duty in the Philippines.

1922
Marries Louise Cromwell Brooks.

1912
Captain MacArthur joins the army general staff in Washington, D.C.

1905
Tours Far East with parents.

1927
Major General MacArthur is named president of the U.S. Olympic Committee.

1930
President Herbert Hoover appoints him army chief of staff.

1934
Philippine government requests MacArthur's services as military adviser.

1942
MacArthurs escape to Australia.

1945
Manila, Bataan, and Corregidor recaptured; Japanese surrender aboard battleship *Missouri;* MacArthur made supreme commander of Allied forces in Japan.

1951
Relieved of command; returns to States; Senate hearings investigate his dismissal.

1938
Son Arthur IV born in Manila on February 21.

1952
MacArthur delivers keynote address at GOP National Convention.

1930	1935	1940	1950	1960	1970

1935
Mother, Pinky MacArthur, dies.

1962
MacArthur's farewell to West Point.

1941
United States enters World War II; withdraws Allied forces to Corregidor and Bataan.

1950
Korean War begins; MacArthur clashes with President Harry Truman.

1964
Dies April 5 and is buried in Norfolk, Virginia.

1932
Bonus Army incident.

1942–1944
Successful battles mark return to the Philippines; becomes a five-star general.

1936
Marries Jean Marie Faircloth.

A Man of Contradictions

Douglas MacArthur was a man of many contradictions. He was a gifted military commander but made incredible miscalculations in estimating the strength of the enemy, mistakes he blamed on others.

MacArthur's ability to recall details and focus on battle plans led to his success against many opponents.

MacArthur was capable of great courage in the face of the enemy. His twenty-two medals, thirteen of them for heroism, outnumber those of any other soldier in American history, yet he was nicknamed "Dugout Doug" for seeking refuge within the fortress of Corregidor while his embattled troops faced enemy fire on the nearby Bataan Peninsula.

He did not hesitate to put the men under his command at risk, but MacArthur had great compassion for those who fell. He could be ruthless as a killer of enemy soldiers, but his attitude toward war was ambivalent, exulting in triumph while pitying the victims of battle, whether friend or foe. Many men serving under him testify they saw tears in his eyes when observing a field strewn with dead and dying.

MacArthur was brilliant when focusing on details of battle plans but often lacked broader comprehension of world events. His memory for facts and figures was amazing. Having seen the terrain of a hillside on his first tour of duty in the Philippines in 1903, for example, he remembered the details when they became crucial to winning a battle forty years later in World War II. This ability to recall and exploit seemingly insignificant details was key to his success against his opponents. He remembered the history of every Japanese unit he

MacArthur accumulated twenty-two medals throughout his career, more than any other soldier in American history.

He read every item written about him, and no reporter who gave an unfavorable account was ever granted an interview again. Historian William Manchester, who met many of the leaders of the day, says, "'Ike' [Dwight D. Eisenhower] asked to be liked, and he was. MacArthur demanded that he be revered, and he wasn't."[1]

MacArthur was both respected and reviled by colleagues, but even his detractors could sing his praises. General George Marshall, who directed U.S. long-range military planning, disliked MacArthur personally but conceded that he was "our most brilliant general."[2] Jonathan Wainwright, an American officer left behind in the Philippines when MacArthur was recalled to Australia during the bitterest fighting on Bataan, still professed loyalty when he said, "I'd follow that man—anywhere—blindfolded."[3]

More than a quarter-century after MacArthur's death, his role in history is still a matter of debate. He is the most highly decorated soldier on record, but was he a great man?

There is no doubt that MacArthur was one of the dominant figures of the first half of the twentieth century. Understanding such a complex individual is not easy, but it is important to understanding some of the most significant events of the century. His actions changed the course of events in such a way that the story of his life marks some of the milestones in world history.

faced in the field, analyzing the type of attack or defense to expect. Yet, at times, immersed in details of his own war plans, he would not concede the importance of other world events.

He was a man who yearned for public adoration, but his manner in dealing with the press guaranteed he would not get it.

1 The Wild West

One might say that Douglas MacArthur spent his entire life in the army, not just as a professional soldier, but from infancy to old age; he was born in one army hospital and died in another. As a child he went to school on army bases and lived in army barracks and officers' quarters. The military was his world; he knew nothing else.

He was born January 26, 1880, at the army arsenal in Little Rock, Arkansas, where his father, Captain Arthur MacArthur, commanded a company of cavalry. Captain MacArthur, a career army officer who had distinguished himself for bravery during the Civil War, had been awarded the Congressional Medal of Honor. Douglas's mother was Mary Pinkney Hardy, called "Pinky" by her husband. She met her future husband at a social affair and fell in love with the dashing young Union officer, much to her family's displeasure because of their ties to the defeated Confederacy.

Six months after Douglas's birth, Captain MacArthur was ordered to take his unit, Company K, to Fort Wingate, located in what at that time was known as the Arizona Territory. The soldiers' assignment was to keep the Navajos on their reservation and protect them from the marauding Apaches of that region.

Douglas's earliest memories were of bugles and the formal rituals of military life;

the fort was his playground. Every afternoon at 5:30 the entire company would assemble within the stockade for the retreat ceremony. The officers appeared in their frock coats with red sashes, tasseled epaulets, and gleaming swords, assembled in neat ranks, resplendent in spiked helmets of black and gold. The post band of several buglers, a fiddler or two, and a drummer pounded out the national anthem. The Stars and Stripes slowly descended the flagstaff and a pack howitzer was fired.

Life was hard on such an isolated military post. Pinky had not grown up expecting to be a military wife. However, if there were times when she wished to be back home, Douglas MacArthur remembered no expression of regret.

Medical care on an isolated military post was primitive at best, and when Douglas and his brothers, Arthur and Malcolm, contracted measles in 1883, Malcolm died. His parents brought Malcolm back to be buried in Pinky's family plot in Virginia. MacArthur remembers, "His loss was a terrible blow to my mother, but it seemed only to increase her devotion to my brother Arthur and myself. This tie was to become one of the dominant factors of my life."[4]

Following the burial of Malcolm, Captain MacArthur, accompanied by his family, returned to duty in the west. This time the post was even more remote: tiny Fort Seldon near the Mexican border. Geronimo and his band of Apaches had refused to accept reservation life or to live peacefully with their neighbors. It was the job of Fort Seldon's troops to guard the fords of the Rio Grande from attack by Geronimo and his men.

What the MacArthurs found when they arrived at Fort Seldon was a bleak scene. A half-dozen adobe buildings in serious disrepair were surrounded by an adobe wall six feet thick and some twelve feet high. The wall cut off an equally bleak view of desert wasteland that stretched to the horizon. Many people would have found such a place depressing, but the frontier offered other rewards. Douglas recalled that these were some of the happiest times of his life: "I learned to ride and shoot before I could walk and talk."[5]

Because Fort Seldon had no school, Pinky tried to introduce her sons to book learning on her own, but frontier life offered

Military life filled MacArthur's childhood memories. His father was a career army officer who received the Congressional Medal of Honor during the Civil War.

distractions that made formal education seem tame in comparison. For example, one day a strange animal came to the water hole and sent the mules and horses into a panicked stampede. It was a camel, survivor of a herd imported by the War Department in 1855 to serve as pack animals in the dry desert emptiness of the Ameri-

Early Lessons

There were many lessons to be learned even in his early years, as Douglas MacArthur tells his readers in his autobiography, Reminiscences.

"The little outpost at Fort Seldon became our home for the next three years.

Company 'K', with its two officers, its assistant surgeon, and forty-six enlisted men comprised the lonely garrison, sheltered in single-story, flat-roofed adobe buildings. It was here I learned to ride and shoot even before I could read or write—indeed, almost before I could walk and talk. My mother, with some help from my father, began the education of her two boys. Our teaching included not only the simple rudiments, but above all else, a sense of obligation. We were to do what was right no matter what the personal sacrifices might be. Our country was always to come first. Two things we must never do: never lie, never tattle.

Life was vivid and exciting for me. In addition to my brother, there was William Highs, the son of the first lieutenant of the company. We were inseparable comrades then, but little did we dream that years later we would be comrades-in-arms on the fields of France. He was my operations officer, G-3 and later my chief of staff in the Rainbow Division during the First World War.

We found much to divert us. There were the visiting officer and mounted details from the cavalry post at Fort Stanton to the east guarding the nearby Mescalero Reservation. There were the bumpy rides on the mule-drawn water wagon that made the daily trip to the Rio Grande several miles west of the post. And toward twilight each evening, the stirring ceremony of retreat, when we would stand at attention as the bugle sounded the lowering of the flag."

After the death of his brother Malcolm to measles, MacArthur's mother became increasingly devoted to Douglas and his brother Arthur (pictured).

can Southwest. The boys were forbidden by their mother to try to lasso it, but try they did, without success.

School for the First Time

When Douglas turned six, Company K was ordered north to Fort Leavenworth, Kansas. For the first time Douglas and his brother headed for the army's Force Public School. Douglas found school boring. Hours were long, rules rigid. Nothing broke the monotony of dry lessons that lacked the excitement of what was even then called the Wild West. "I found it no substitute for the color and excitement of the frontier West,"[6] MacArthur recalled in his autobiography.

In September 1896 the MacArthur family was transferred to Fort Sam Houston in San Antonio, Texas, the largest military fort in the west, where Douglas was enrolled at the West Texas Military Academy. As a military school, battle tactics and strategy were part of the academy's curriculum. A lesson about the Revolutionary War, for example, included a full discussion of all the conflict's battles. Relating historical events to modern military training helped Douglas become excited about learning.

The Civil War was of special interest because Douglas's own father had been a hero in one of the hardest-fought battles, at Missionary Ridge in Tennessee. He had charged up a hill amid heavy enemy fire and planted the Union Jack at the summit, inspiring others to follow. At age seventeen, he had been cited for bravery by General Philip Sheridan and awarded the Congressional Medal of Honor, the nation's highest military award.

Douglas liked to imagine himself dashing into battle. He thought of no other future besides a career in the army, nor of any college but the U.S. Military Academy at West Point, New York. His father pointed out that to enter the academy, top grades were just as important as the ability to ride a horse and shoot straight. This lecture from his father helped change Douglas into a conscientious student.

MacArthur loved competition of all kinds. He made the school's football and baseball teams and became tennis champion on his campus. He also enjoyed competing against other students for top grades and graduated from West Texas Military Academy with a 96.67 grade average.

Douglas planned to enroll at West Point immediately. He had never considered not being accepted, although he had to pass physical and academic exams and be formally recommended by a member of Congress from Wisconsin, where his family had registered their legal residence. This admission process would be the toughest competition of all. But though Douglas passed the entrance exam with excellent scores and secured the recommendations of a considerable number of well-known people to present to members of Congress, his name was not on the final list of appointees presented to West Point. MacArthur always would believe his rejection was engineered by President Grover Cleveland, a Democrat, because of his family's Republican loyalties. It was an excuse he could live with since it did not reflect on his own merit.

But he would try again. MacArthur and his mother moved to Milwaukee to be with his grandfather, a well-known judge in Wisconsin. Here Douglas could cram for the entrance exam and prepare himself for next year's competition while his grandfather worked to enlist a congressional supporter for his appointment. "I never worked harder in my life,"[7] MacArthur later remembered of his efforts that year.

On the day he was to take the entrance test, he was extremely nervous. He had hardly slept the night before. His mother accompanied him to the test site and urged him to "Be self-confident . . . even if you don't make it, you will know that you have done your best. Now go to it."[8]

He passed the written exams with high marks, but received the disappointing news that he had failed the physical. The examining doctor told him that he had a slight curvature of the spine, which could be corrected with exercise. Douglas MacArthur spent hours working with barbells to build his strength and strapping himself into a back brace to help correct his spinal curvature. Because of his conscientious workouts, he corrected the problem in less than six months, in time to report for duty at the college of his choice, the U.S. Military Academy.

West Point

On the afternoon of June 13, 1899, Douglas MacArthur and his mother arrived by train at West Point. Douglas's older brother had recently graduated from the U.S. Naval Academy in Annapolis, Maryland, and was already assigned to sea duty. Since MacArthur had never owned a home, it now seemed only natural to Mrs. MacArthur that she should take up residency in a hotel near the academy so that she could be close to the only member of the family not on active duty. Her presence, though, did not seem natural to the other cadets, who wondered about a student who had to bring his mother with him to school.

There was an established custom at West Point that first-year cadets, known as plebes, were put through a ritual of hazing. This amounted to a physical test to see if the newcomers were strong enough to be cadets. Although hazing was not offi-

Life at West Point

Geoffrey Perret, in his book Old Soldiers Never Die, *gives an accurate account of life at West Point for young Douglas.*

"During his time as a cadet Douglas was paid five hundred dollars a year, more or less what a skilled worker of the time earned. He had to remain within the limits of West Point almost his entire four years. He could ride a horse for a distance of up to six miles away, but he could not stop, dismount or speak to anyone. Or he might take a boat trip on the Hudson, but he couldn't tie up on shore or talk to anyone on another boat. At the end of two years he would receive a ten-week leave, then return for two more cloistered years. The West Point system created a sense of isolation that made it easier to model youthful clay into the kind of Army officer the Academic Board believed the country needed.

Douglas MacArthur was luckier than most cadets. The West Point Hotel stood within the academy grounds. He would have an outsider to talk to, to confide in, to turn to for advice. He was able to meet his mother most afternoons at a bench outside the hotel for half an hour. Cadets got used to seeing mother and son walking around Trophy Point deep in conversation. On days when he could not leave the barracks, Pinky crossed the Plain and paced up and down the sidewalks outside the barracks with Douglas."

cially condoned by the academy's staff, the ritual was generally accepted as normal pranks young men played on each other.

MacArthur was a prime target for hazing. Some of the cadets resented Douglas's calm, confident air, which they interpreted as arrogance. Being the son of a well-known general also set him apart. The upperclassmen resolved to break his reserve and make him beg for relief.

One evening he was ordered to report to a tent on the drill field occupied by six upperclassmen. In his biography of MacArthur, Norman Richards reports that "the leader made scathing remarks about Douglas' mother being at West Point, called him a snob, a spoiled brat, a show-off for having scored such high marks on his entrance examination."[9] Instead of losing his temper, MacArthur remained silent.

MacArthur was told that he had two choices, to submit to physical punishment or face a match with the head of the cadet's boxing team. MacArthur knew what that meant. He was not afraid of a fistfight, but he had heard the results of other such matches. As soon as a plebe finished a bout with one member of the boxing team, he would have to take on the whole team until he was knocked unconscious. He decided to accept whatever other punishment the upperclassmen would dole out.

The torture started innocently enough with an order to do deep knee bends. Then he was told to do them faster and faster. After two hours he pitched forward on his face, unconscious. He was revived with a bucket of water.

As soon as he revived, he was forced to do pushups. Another hour passed. His muscles ached. He could hardly breathe. Again and again he was taunted by the upperclassmen, who asked him why he was trying to be such a hero.

Finally at dawn his tormentors gave up and he was sent back to his room. He was wracked with convulsions and stomach cramps so severe that his roommate urged him to report to the infirmary. Instead he reported for duty the next day as if nothing had happened.

Word of the hazing reached the officers in charge of discipline and academic standards at West Point. Because this seemed to have been a particularly brutal incident, an inquiry was undertaken in which MacArthur was called upon to testify. He refused to tell who had done the hazing. Through his silence, he earned the respect of those upperclassmen. He would never be called a mama's boy again.

Family Ties

In his book American Caesar, *historian William Manchester explains the profound influence of MacArthur's mother in forming his character.*

"His mother was to remain close to him until he was in his fifties, but her influence on him was naturally greatest in those early years. If his father provided him with an example of manliness and a love of language, Pinky contributed other qualities that would distinguish him to the end of his life. Some were superficial: the courtly manner he acquired and the fastidiousness which, she would later tell him, he had inherited from his plantation forebears. Others were more subtle, because she herself was a complex woman, being both meek and tough, petulant and sentimental, charming and emotional. Under her mannered, pretty exterior she was cool, practical, and absolutely determined that her children would not only match but surpass the achievements of her father-in-law and her husband."

He had earned respect, but as one of his friends later said, "To know MacArthur is to love him or hate him. You just can't like him."[10]

Although he already had the stern disposition he later applied to military command, there was a more human side to his bearing. He fell in love frequently. One classmate counted that MacArthur had been engaged no less than eight times. On each occasion his mother intervened, and MacArthur never seemed to be so desperately smitten that he felt it worth an argument with the strong-willed Pinky.

MacArthur ranked at the top of his class academically every year. He did not seem to study hard, but his concentration was intense. Each year he received the highest rank available to him: senior corporal in his sophomore year, first sergeant as a second classman, and in his last year as a first classman, the crowning glory of first captain.

When graduation day came June 11, 1903, he was voted the cadet most likely to succeed. No one would have guessed to what heights he would rise.

As a cadet at West Point, MacArthur received the highest ranks available to him. His classmates voted him the cadet most likely to succeed.

2 A Young Officer's Training

Second Lieutenant Douglas MacArthur would have preferred serving in a cavalry unit, if only for the drama and glory it might offer, but there were few places left in the world where men on horseback could charge into battle. Cavalry units were already being phased out of the army, so he was assigned to the Corps of Engineers, where at least there would be more chance for advancement.

He spent the two months between graduation and his first assignment with his mother and father in San Francisco, where General MacArthur was serving as commander of the U.S. Army Division of the Pacific. Even on vacation Douglas MacArthur managed a dramatic bit of action to add to his personal record. The MacArthurs were living on the grounds of Fort Mason when a prisoner escaped from a work detail on the site. The escapee was armed with a scythe and considered dangerous. Search parties were organized.

"It was none of my business, but I had tracked trails too often with the Apaches not to pick up on this one. His hiding place was easy to locate, and I had him covered before he had a chance to make a move. When I turned him over to the guard, he just spat at me and snarled, 'You damn West Pointer,'"[11] MacArthur recalled.

This was the remark the young lieutenant was proud to record in his autobiography.

Another MacArthur in the Philippines

MacArthur's first tour of duty took him to the Philippines, where he immediately fell under the tropical spell of the islands. As he put it years later, "The languorous laze that seemed to glamorize even the most routine chores of life, the fun-loving men, the moonbeam delicacy of its lovely women, fastened me with a grip that has never relaxed."[12]

As an engineer, MacArthur supervised the construction of docks far from the glamour of the capital city of Manila. He was put to work on Guimaris Island located at the mouth of Iloilo Harbor. Again an incident occurred that added to his image as a hero. Required to procure pilings for the project, he led a small detachment to cut timber in the jungle forest. As he later wrote:

In spite of my frontier training, I became careless and allowed myself to be waylaid on a narrow jungle trail by two desperadoes, one on each side. Like all frontiersmen, I was expert with a pistol. I dropped them both dead in their tracks, but not before one blazed away at me with his antiquated rifle. The slug tore through my campaign hat.[13]

MacArthur survived the attack unhurt, but he was not spared a serious bout of malaria. He was sent back to Manila for better medical care, but for several months he was wracked with fever and nausea. MacArthur resented the required bed rest because he worried it would delay his advancement as an officer. MacArthur used the enforced idleness to good purpose, though. After several letters to the division commander of his unit, he was permitted in March 1904 to take the examination for first lieutenant.

One of the questions on the exam posed the hypothetical problem of how best to defend a harbor with a given number of troops. MacArthur answered with detailed military logistics. The follow-up question asked what he would do if all the troops were withdrawn. MacArthur's answer showed that he had a sense of humor: "First, I'd round up all the sign painters in the community and put them to work making signs reading: BEWARE—THIS HARBOR IS MINED. After that I'd get down on my hands and knees and pray. Then I'd go out and fight like hell."[14]

First Weeks in Manila

In Old Soldiers Never Die, *biographer Geoffrey Perret gives this account of MacArthur's lifestyle during his first assignment to the Philippines.*

"Douglas had the company of nearly a dozen of his classmates during the leisurely five-and-a-half week voyage to Manila. When he arrived in the islands, he discovered that the enervating heat and humidity meant drilling before sun came up. The day's work was done mainly between breakfast and noon. Lunch was followed by a siesta until 4:00 P.M. Then came the ceremony of retreat. Fastidious officers such as MacArthur changed their uniforms four times a day and took three showers. But MacArthur was not only fastidious; he attached enormous importance to appearances. If he could not do something stylishly, he chose not to do it at all. Many young officers stationed in and around Manila went into the city most evenings to enjoy themselves. MacArthur went only if he could afford a carriage and driver to take him to town and return him to quarters. And when MacArthur was out on the town, he wore his best white uniform."

In October, MacArthur returned to San Francisco wearing the silver bars of a first lieutenant; three months later he received new orders. He was to proceed to Tokyo, Japan, and report to General Arthur MacArthur for appointment as aide-de-camp on his staff.

World Travel

The elder MacArthur had been ordered to observe and report on the activities of the Japanese military during the Russo-Japanese War. Once that war ended, Arthur MacArthur was further ordered to survey military conditions throughout the Far East. During the next nine months, the general, Pinky, and Lieutenant MacArthur traveled through parts of the world entirely unknown to most Americans. This tour gave the young Douglas MacArthur a glimpse of the role of diplomacy in world affairs, and he came to understand that more could be learned about countries in times of peace than in wartime.

This was a time of relative luxury, and travel was slow and elegant. Young MacArthur and his parents visited military bases, dined with royalty, and viewed lifestyles totally different from theirs. As Norman Finkelstein relates, "From Japan to India, from Ceylon to Siam, they saw wondrous sights—the Khyber Pass, Shanghai, Hong Kong, Saigon, and China."[15]

It was a time for learning, and no lessons were forgotten. MacArthur remembers that "I met all the great commanders; Oyama, Kuroki, Nogi, and the brilliant Admiral Heihachiro Togo—those grim, taciturn, and aloof men of iron character and unshakable purpose. It was here I first encountered the boldness and courage of the Nipponese soldier. His almost fanatical belief and reverence for his Emperor impressed me indelibly."[16]

These years were a time of friendship between the two countries, and trust between MacArthur and some of the Japanese officers he met. He asked one Japanese signal officer he had befriended what types of codes were used to transmit operational messages. After some hesitation over a bowl of sake, the Japanese officer confided that the most secret messages were sent without change in the Japanese language. No foreigner, he said, would understand it. Many years later, during World War II, vital knowledge of the Japanese language helped U.S. intelligence officers break codes the enemy thought to be secure.

Promotion

When the MacArthurs returned from their travels, Arthur MacArthur was promoted to major general, although he had been hoping to be appointed as army chief of staff. When that appointment went to someone else, he decided, at age sixty-four, to retire. While his career was ending, his son's career was on the rise.

In the fall of 1906, Douglas MacArthur was sent to study at the Engineer's School of Application in Washington, D.C. He requested permission to visit the Panama Canal, which was under construction and would soon link the Atlantic and Pacific Oceans. He appreciated the opportunity to study the huge engineering, supply, and sanitation problems presented by such a project. MacArthur now realized that the canal was vital to America's military. Naval

The Panama Canal was vital to the American military. It allowed troop movement between the Atlantic and Pacific Oceans in case of political crises.

forces of the United States would no longer have to be divided between the Atlantic and Pacific Oceans. Moreover, troop movements between the hemispheres would be made easier in the event of political crises.

Upon his return to Washington, MacArthur was assigned as an aide to President Theodore Roosevelt. In that position he had the opportunity to meet American political leaders and foreign heads of state to hear their assessments of world affairs. The time allowed MacArthur to learn lessons more valuable than courses at West Point provided. The young military officer gained a view of the complexities of the world as a whole for the first time.

For the next five years his assignments were routine, but his ability to take the ini-

tiative and get jobs done brought Douglas MacArthur to the attention of his commanding officers. By February 1911, he had been promoted to the rank of captain. Word of the promotion was relayed to his delighted father.

General MacArthur had returned to his home in Milwaukee on retiring. On September 5, 1912, his old regiment, the 24th of Wisconsin, was to hold its fiftieth reunion. Ninety veterans who had served under him during the Civil War were still living. In spite of ill health, Arthur MacArthur had agreed to speak to the group. Although Pinky urged him to save his strength and decline the invitation, the thought of being back in uniform in front of his troops was a strong incentive to attend.

Biographer William Manchester, in American Caesar, *explains the problems the young man had to face in the care of his mother following his father's death.*

"A much sharper break with his childhood came the following year with the death of his father. It greatly exacerbated what had until now been a minor problem, the demands of his mother. Douglas and his brother remained in Milwaukee after the funeral, trying to comfort and reassure her. They failed. Exhibiting symptoms of a grief syndrome not unknown among the bereaved, she insisted—for the first time but by no means the last time—that she was desperately ill. One of them would have to care for her. Since Arthur III was serving aboard ship, it would have to be his brother."

The old general stepped to the podium, standing as straight and tall as he had as a young recruit. He spoke of the accomplishments of the "indomitable regiment." Then suddenly his face turned ashen white. His breath came in short gasps and he collapsed. At once a doctor rushed to his side. The unit's chaplain began to recite the Lord's Prayer, and the ninety men who had followed him in battle knelt and joined in the prayer. By the time the prayer ended Arthur MacArthur was dead. His son was not prepared for the loss of his father. "My whole world changed that night. Never have I been able to heal the wound in my heart,"[17] he said.

Training on Another Front

When the grief-stricken MacArthur was ordered back to Washington, he took his widowed mother to live with him. He had been expecting another tour of duty overseas, but was instead selected, at the unusually young age of thirty-two, as a member of the army general staff. Most young officers in such a position would have listened quietly to discussion in the staff meetings and refrained from arguing with the more experienced officers. MacArthur, on the other hand, took time to write lengthy reports of his own on various subjects, offering his own opinions, whether they matched the views of the majority or not. This practice generated resentment on the part of some of the older officers. Yet because of his ability to analyze problems, he was handpicked by Army Chief of Staff General Leonard Wood for his next job.

Early in 1913 Mexico was plunged into political turmoil when General Victoriano Huerta seized control of the government. Numerous atrocities had been attributed to Huerta and his followers. The president of Mexico, Francisco Madero, who was encouraging the passage of laws that would move Mexico closer to a democracy, was assassinated. Outraged, President Woodrow Wilson withheld recognition of the new Mexican government, but Germany agreed to supply Huerta with the arms needed to keep him in power. A German ship carrying 260 machine guns and 15 million rounds of ammunition set sail for the east coast port of Veracruz. The U.S. Navy blockaded the port to prevent the German ship from docking. War between Germany and the United States seemed imminent, and General Wood needed an advance man on the scene to keep him abreast of developments. He sent Captain Douglas MacArthur to Veracruz to assess the situation.

When MacArthur arrived, he learned from the American commander on the scene, Brigadier General Frederick Funston, that if Huerta continued his guerrilla tactics, Funston was prepared to move south, closer to the battleground that was taking Mexican lives every day. Although he had men on the scene in Veracruz, Funston would need a way to move his troops quickly through the countryside. A railroad line on a direct route to Mexico City could easily be commandeered by U.S. troops, but there was a problem. There were hundreds of boxcars in Veracruz, but no locomotives.

MacArthur devised a plan to get the needed engines. He had heard rumors that five locomotives were hidden about forty miles south of Veracruz. He intended to locate them so that they would be available if the need arose. Without informing his superiors, he planned a one-man reconnaissance mission to find the engines. He recruited three Mexican railroad workers by offering them $150 each to help him.

MacArthur left Veracruz on foot: "I was in military uniform with no effort at disguise and with absolutely nothing on me in addition to my clothes, except my identification tag, a small Bible, and my pistol belt. I found my engineer with a hand car at the appointed place."[18]

They set off down the track in the darkness of night. For the first ten miles everything went smoothly, but at the town of Jamapa they found that the railroad bridge across the Jamapa River had been blown up. They concealed the handcar under shrubbery alongside the track for use on the return trip. After searching the bank of the river, they found a small boat, which they used to cross the river. Once across the river, they located two ponies and followed the rail line past Paso del Toro.

Act of Bravery

The other two members of the team were waiting for them with another handcar. MacArthur skirted villages because he was certain that an American army officer on a handcar would be captured instantly: "At every town we reached, I took one man and left the car which was run through by the other two. I fastened myself by a lashing to the man acting as my guide,"[19] he wrote.

They reached the town of Alvarado about one o'clock in the morning. There they found the locomotives they were looking for. Of the five engines, two were switch engines and of no use, but the other three were usable. American forces easily could capture the equipment at a later time if it should be needed.

Returning with the information was not as easy as he had hoped. On the way back they were intercepted by five armed men. Pumping the handcar on the tracks as fast as they could, MacArthur and his Mexican companions tried to outdistance the bandits as the enemy opened fire. MacArthur returned shots, and two men went down. His companions tried to flee, but MacArthur commanded them to keep going if they wanted to be paid.

Once more they were stopped, this time by fifteen armed men on horseback. MacArthur was knocked down by the rush of the horsemen. Pistol in hand, he picked off four of the horsemen, but not before three bullets ripped holes through his uniform. He was unharmed but one member of his railroad crew was wounded in the shoulder. Fortunately for MacArthur and his crew, the men on horseback did not pursue them.

At Paso del Toro they abandoned the handcar and found the ponies where they had left them. They rode at full gallop to the river's edge, where the boat was still hidden. The wounded man was now so weak from loss of blood that MacArthur

MacArthur used a handcar (such as the one pictured) to search for locomotives needed to move troops throughout Mexico.

The Importance of Being Noticed

Geoffrey Perret highlights MacArthur's personal style in his book Old Soldiers Never Die.

"Life in the field brought out a different side to MacArthur. He began to dress in an extravagant, eye-catching style that screamed, 'Look at me!' The most noticeable thing about him was not just his good looks but his determination to be noticed. He had arrived at West Point wearing a huge Stetson (cowboy hat) as if he had just arrived from Texas, not Milwaukee. Over time his choice of headgear would provide a chapter on fashion in itself. At Veracruz he wore a slightly battered campaign hat. Nothing much to impress there. But below that he wore his captain's bars sideways on his shirt collar, a cardigan that stretched to his knees, a brightly colored silk cravat around his neck, and stuck in his mouth was a pipe. Here then, was the emergence of another MacArthur, the peacock strutting among pigeons. He had taken the relaxation of dress regulations in the field and run with them until he scored what seemed to him to be a touchdown."

With his campaign hat and pipe, MacArthur took the relaxation of dress regulations in the field to a new level.

had to carry him to the boat. Quietly they eased the craft into the water. Silence was crucial, since they were close to rebel lines, where trained soldiers were ready to open fire if they were detected. Just short of the far side of the river, the boat hit a snag and sank. MacArthur had to use all his strength to keep the wounded man's head above water as they swam to safety. It was daylight before they located their first handcar and rolled in close to Veracruz, where they crossed into friendly territory.

An Award Denied

MacArthur did not receive the Medal of Honor for which General Wood recommended him. In American Caesar, *William Manchester explains the deliberations of the awards board and MacArthur's reaction.*

"War was not declared. Wood did not take the field, and he never reached the White House, but the Vera Cruz incident discloses much about MacArthur: his ingenuity, his eye for terrain, his personal bravery, and his toadying to superiors. Later he would bestow similar presidential benedictions [flattery] on other men in a position to give him a leg up. The aftermath is revealing in another way. Wood recommended him for the Medal of Honor, noting that the expedition, which had been undertaken 'at the risk of his life' and 'under his own initiative,' showed 'enterprise and courage worthy of high commendation.' An awards board rejected the recommendation on the grounds that since Funston hadn't known about the reconnaissance, decorating Captain MacArthur 'might encourage any other staff officer, under similar conditions, to ignore the local commander, possibly interfering with the latter's plans with reference to the enemy.' That was absurd, and the captain was entitled to resent it, but he went further, submitting an official memorandum protesting 'the rigid narrow-mindedness and lack of imagination' of the awards board. It availed him nothing, merely strengthening the convictions of those who saw him as a temperamental pleader."

When the full story of MacArthur's unsanctioned escapade reached General Wood, he recommended the young captain for the Congressional Medal of Honor. Because MacArthur had been acting without orders, however, the medal was not awarded. This was a disappointment to MacArthur, who had always wanted to equal his father's record. However, he was promoted to the rank of major and continued to serve on the general staff.

The conflict in Mexico did not spill across its borders, and subsided in 1916 after inconclusive skirmishes with U.S. troops. Meanwhile, a disastrous conflict was brewing in Europe that would prove to be a much more difficult test for MacArthur.

3 The World at War

By late 1914 much of Europe was engulfed in World War I. The United States was officially a neutral noncombatant, but Germany's unrestricted submarine warfare on all shipping finally brought the United States into the war on the side of the Allies (primarily Britain, France, and Russia), against the Central Powers of Germany, Austria, and Turkey.

When Congress finally declared war on Germany on April 6, 1917, the United States did not have an army large enough to fight a major war. There was no law to allow the drafting of men into the military, so the U.S. secretary of war, Newton Baker, needed to encourage volunteers. Major Douglas MacArthur was given the job of handling press relations. In that role he arranged interviews with various well-known figures, both in military circles and in politics, who pointed out that it was the duty of men to protect the honor of their country. In press releases he continued to campaign for bills before Congress authorizing expansion of the army.

The first decision by the War Office was to induct men into the army by lottery. Here, too, MacArthur played a key part. Through numerous editorials that he contributed to newspapers throughout the country, he built public support for the Selective Service Act passed by Congress on May 18, 1917.

Next came the question of whether to call up the National Guard to fight overseas. Baker and MacArthur went to President Wilson to argue the merits of sending units of the National Guard to Europe. Wilson agreed that the plan was reasonable, but he wondered how he could fairly decide which troops would be sent. The National Guard is made up of units specifically recruited from individual states with the purpose of keeping order in that state. Would it be fair to send the California troops to the front first, instead of soldiers from Maine?

MacArthur proposed a solution. A division containing National Guardsmen from every state in the Union, he suggested, would stir national pride and enthusiasm. It would officially be known as the 42nd Division, but as it was composed of men from twenty-six states and the District of Columbia, it was informally known as the Rainbow Division, since its membership spanned the nation, from the Atlantic to the Pacific, like a giant rainbow. It was a true citizen army, twenty-seven thousand strong, with regular army officers only in positions of top leadership.

As its creator, MacArthur was the natural choice to head the division, and with that appointment, he skipped two ranks to become a colonel. MacArthur accepted the position on one condition, that he be assigned to the infantry, not as an engineer. As an infantry soldier, he would be in the thick of the fighting, where he felt he could best serve his country as a leader of men in combat.

As commander of the Rainbow Division, MacArthur would be involved in every aspect of running the unit, from training the men to expediting the gathering of equipment. There was no time to lose, and they must be prepared.

Over There

On October 18, 1917, the USS *Covington* docked at the port of Hoboken, New Jersey,

to take on troops, including the Rainbow Division. The *Covington* would be part of a large convoy braving the dangers of both sea and hostile submarines. The trip across the Atlantic Ocean took thirteen days. Forty miles from their destination, the port of St. Nazaire at the mouth of the Loire River, the ship ran aground. Then an enemy submarine was sighted. Seven patrol boats answered the SOS to protect the transport until it could be floated free. It was not an auspicious start to MacArthur's command, and further trouble lay just ahead.

Shortly after the Rainbow Division arrived on French soil, MacArthur received an order from General John J. Pershing,

First Attack

In his autobiography, MacArthur gives his own account of the Rainbow Division's acid test—the attack.

"Zero hour was five o'clock plus five minutes. The French had moved in their artillery, preparing to commence fire at five minutes short of zero hour. There was a cold drizzle, the air was sharp with coming storm, the mud ankle deep. The Germans sensed the operation, and forty batteries of their guns opened with deadly accurate fury. Our casualties began to mount. I began to feel uneasy. You never really know about men at such a time. They were not professionals. Few of them had ever been under fire. I decided to walk the line, hoping that my presence might comfort the men.

Behind our lines, a few scattered batteries had been sporadically trying to hold down the enemy fire. They had not been successful. But as my watch hit zero hour minus five, the night trembled with the thunderous belch of sixty batteries. As fast as sweating gunners could throw in their shells, the guns flashed with fire. In the fast graying twilight I could see pillars of smoke and flame shoot skyward from the German salient."

As commander of the Rainbow Division, MacArthur was responsible for the training of the men and control over their equipment.

commander in chief of the American Expeditionary Force. The 42nd Division would be broken up, its men used as replacements for other divisions. In MacArthur's view, his troops were to be used as cannon fodder.

Furious, MacArthur immediately wired the secretary of war:

PERSHING INTENDS CHOP UP RAINBOW FOR REPLACEMENTS STOP MEANS RUIN OF CRACK DIVISION TRAINED TO WORK AS TEAM AND DESTROY MORALE OF TROOPS PROUD OF BEING RAINBOW MEN STOP URGE PROMPT ACTION TO SAVE THE DIVISION SPONSORED BY PRESIDENT WILSON HIMSELF MACARTHUR.[20]

Pershing was angry that MacArthur had dared to jump the chain of command. The division was left intact, but from

Animosity between General John J. Pershing (pictured) and MacArthur began when Pershing tried to disband the Rainbow Division.

that moment on, MacArthur and Pershing shared a mutual animosity, displayed in public as well as privately.

In the Trenches

When orders finally came for the Rainbow Division to move to the front line, in the Meuse Valley, the men were as combat-ready as possible, but conditions they were forced to endure in the field were horrendous. They had left home with plenty of equipment, but much of their spare clothing and supplies had been requisitioned by general headquarters for use by other undersupplied divisions. The winter of 1917–1918 was one of the harshest ever recorded in the Meuse Valley, and some of the men of the 42nd did not even have coats or army boots. The men were housed in cold farmhouses, often along with cows and pigs.

Once he and his men had arrived in the trenches, MacArthur wanted to survey for himself the ground between the opposing lines, known as no-man's-land. It was territory that often changed hands more than once during a single skirmish. He arranged to join a French patrol on a raid to seize prisoners for interrogation. The French commander was shocked: "It is unheard of for a commanding officer to take such a risk." MacArthur argued, "I cannot fight them [the Germans] if I cannot see them."[21]

Over the Top

On his first encounter with the enemy, MacArthur followed the French officer's lead. At a signal the Allied force crawled out of their trenches and set off across the battle-scarred no-man's-land. Cutting through tangled rolls of barbed wire, the men crawled forward on their stomachs as silently as possible, but were detected by a German sentry, who gave the alert. Flares were launched. Machine-gun fire ripped across the lines. The French troops leaped into shell holes or ditches for cover. Many did not make it in time. The firing was fierce until a grenade thrown into the German lines scored a direct hit.

Men struggled and grunted in the darkness, stabbing one another in brutal hand-to-hand combat, pressing handguns against heads or ribs, forced to decide in

First Training

D. Clayton James quotes MacArthur in volume 1 of his biography, The Years of MacArthur, *describing the arrival of the troops on French soil and early training regimen.*

"MacArthur observed that 'the division worked day and night. . . . There were no leave, passes were limited, officers and men fared alike.' The days were long for everyone. Many of the soldiers being in poor physical condition at the start and knowing little about military ways despite their membership in the National Guard. The mornings were spent on close and extended-order drills, physical exercising, and bayonet practice, while the afternoons were devoted to instruction in schools of the soldier and the company, care of weapons, target practice, sentinel duties, and a host of other subjects basic to the combat soldier's training. Specialized instruction was given to men assigned to artillery, engineer, signal, machine gun, sanitation, ammunition, field hospital, and ambulance units."

Under MacArthur, soldiers engaged in a strict regimen of physical exercise, bayonet practice, care of weapons, and in the schooling of the soldier.

an instant whether to kill a man or take him prisoner. A German colonel rushed from his dugout, and MacArthur poked him in the back with his swagger stick. The German instantly surrendered.

The skirmish finally ended with German prisoners taken. The French, with MacArthur beside them, returned to their lines as dawn was lighting a desolate and shell-pocked field of action. MacArthur earned the praise of those who had witnessed his bravery under fire, and he later was awarded a Silver Star for his actions that night.

The Taking of Châtillon

This was but the first of many encounters MacArthur had with the enemy. Doughboys, as Allied infantrymen were known, called him the "Fighting Dude," because of his flamboyant manner of dress. The Germans believed he led a charmed life, but all knew it would take more than bravado to achieve victory. General Pershing was sending all available troops against German bunkers located high above the Meuse River, a fortified position from which to de-

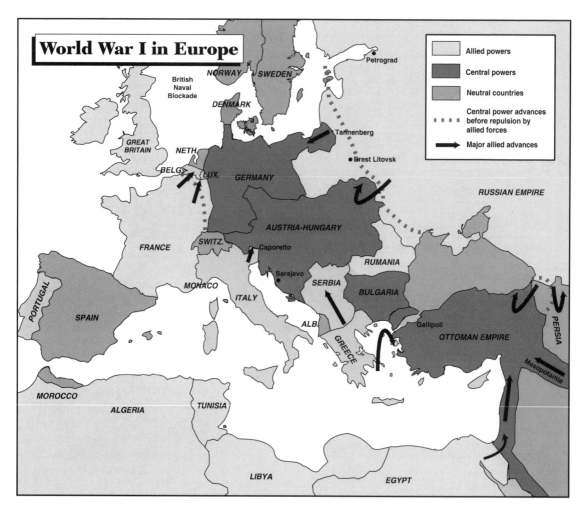

World War I in Europe

Allied powers

Central powers

Neutral countries

Central power advances before repulsion by allied forces

Major allied advances

Petrograd

NORWAY   SWEDEN

British Naval Blockade

DENMARK

Tannenberg

GREAT BRITAIN

NETH.

Brest Litovsk

BELG.   LUX.   GERMANY

RUSSIAN EMPIRE

FRANCE   SWITZ.   AUSTRIA-HUNGARY

Caporetto

RUMANIA

PORTUGAL   MONACO   Sarajevo   SERBIA

ITALY   BULGARIA

SPAIN   ALB.   Gallipoli   PERSIA

GREECE   OTTOMAN EMPIRE

Mesopotamia

MOROCCO

ALGERIA   TUNISIA

LIBYA   EGYPT

In volume 1 of D. Clayton James's The Years of MacArthur, *Major General Charles Menoher assesses the training of the Rainbow Division.*

"By early summer the 42nd Division was in [General Charles] Menoher's opinion, 'a complete, compact, cohesive, single unit, which ran like a well oiled machine. The Division was privileged to plume itself more or less on its excellent staff work,' which was spearheaded by MacArthur, 'a most brilliant officer.' The soldiers were beginning to perform like veterans: raids were conducted with precision and savage effectiveness. German attacks were countered with fierce resistance and seldom caught the Rainbow troops by surprise. An indication of the division's growing efficiency was the fact that only sixty-two casualties were suffered in May in eleven German gas bombardments, involving yperite and palite gases. . . . At Luneville many Americans at first viewed the box respirators and gas masks nonchalantly, but after heavy gassing that first month, they quickly learned the value of anti-gas equipment."

fend the crucial railroad line that supplied Berlin. Pershing ordered MacArthur and his men to take the hill, known as Châtillon, on the east flank of the Allied lines. MacArthur saw the assignment as a challenge. His reply was, "If this brigade does not capture Châtillon you can publish a casualty list of the entire brigade with the brigade commander's name at the top."[22] MacArthur's statement almost proved prophetic.

Even before the attack on the well-fortified hill began, clouds of mustard gas launched by the Germans swept toward them. Men doubled over gasping for breath. The men struggled on, snaking from one shell crater to another. It was a bloody battle, but in the end Châtillon was taken by the Allies. Casualties were heavy: The Allies were left with only 300 men and 6 officers of the original force of 1,450 men and 25 officers.

One-Star General

MacArthur kept up regular correspondence with his mother despite the difficulties posed by the war. In one letter MacArthur noted that he had been recommended by Pershing for promotion to brigadier general. Without MacArthur's knowledge, Pinky's response was to apply

The Fighting Dude

MacArthur's un-orthodox attire is well described in the Army Times Editors' book Banners and the Glory.

"In spite of the hardships they were all enduring, MacArthur became a rallying figure, a Dude, a flamboyant character, smoking expensive cigars, clad in a black turtle-neck sweater and a short, Mackinac-type overcoat. He refused to wear the regulation steel helmet (because it 'hurt' his head) or carry a gas mask (which 'hampered' him)—unbelievable personal carelessness in this man of contradictions, which he would not tolerate in subordinates. He was armed solely with a riding crop."

political pressure to hasten MacArthur's advancement. Mrs. MacArthur, never hesitant to intervene in her son's behalf, wrote Secretary of the Army Newton Baker: "Even if my boy fails to win promotion, I shall always feel that he has made good." She followed this with a letter to General Pershing reminding him of MacArthur's record at West Point, ending with: "I feel I am placing my entire life in your hands." [23] Pinky doubtless wanted her son home as well, but that would not happen right away.

The Armistice

Fighting in World War I ended with the signing of the armistice (truce) by the Allies and the Central Powers on November 11, 1918, but MacArthur's men were not sent home immediately. The Rainbow Division was selected, along with three other divisions, for the occupation of postwar Germany.

Consequently, MacArthur and those of the Rainbow troops who had survived the fighting did not return to the United States until the spring of 1919, exactly eighteen months after the convoy had departed Hoboken. The first waves of returning soldiers had been greeted by crowds and ticker-tape parades; the Rainbow Division was virtually ignored. When the ship docked, the pier was vacant. No crowds were waiting. No bands were playing. No flags were waving. One small boy asked if the men had been to France. He was told that this was the glorious Rainbow Division but he had no idea what that meant. The soldiers turned to each other. They shook hands, hugged, and said good-bye. It was the end of the Rainbow.

4 Back to West Point

The talents that served MacArthur so well in wartime—the ability to inspire troops and organize a large unit—proved useful in peacetime as well. MacArthur's record of leadership of the Rainbow Division, as well as his personal bravery, earned him the post of superintendent of the U.S. Military Academy. It was a job that brought with it plenty of hard work as well as prestige. In the words of General Peyton March, the army chief of staff, MacArthur's job would be to "bring the academy up to date, modernize the course of study, outlaw hazing, and reorganize the whole institution." [24]

MacArthur and his mother moved into the superintendent's house on June 12, 1919. Pinky was now sixty-seven years old and at times in poor health, but as strong an influence on her son as ever. When he complained of the difficulties he had to face, his mother was always there to give support, telling him that he had been chosen for the assignment because no one else could do the job.

Not all the staff was as supportive as his mother was, resistant to too much change made too quickly. MacArthur restored the academic program, which had been stripped during the war, to a four-year course of study. He expanded and enriched the liberal arts curriculum, establishing new departments of history, economics, and government. He modernized instruction in the sciences, bringing in top instructors to teach the latest developments.

Some faculty objected to requirements that cadets study literature, saying such courses were irrelevant to military instruction. MacArthur's reply was, "We are not training military weapons here—we are training military minds. Without a solid grounding in English, no officer can grasp or communicate the subtleties and complexities of international conflicts in the twentieth century. The pen, sir, is *still* mightier than the sword." [25]

Although MacArthur was superintendent, his plans had to be approved by West Point's academic board. MacArthur used every trick he knew in order to obtain the board's approval. Instead of calling meetings in the morning, he scheduled them for 4:30 P.M.: "I want the so-and-so's to come here hungry—I'll keep them here until I get what I want!" [26] A sufficient majority of the board eventually saw things MacArthur's way and allowed him to go ahead with his plans.

MacArthur also emphasized the importance of sports in producing well-rounded officers. He made physical training and intramural sports compulsory for officers and faculty as well as cadets.

He brought back the honor system to the academy, insisting that "West Point men have to be clean, live clean, and think clean." [27] And MacArthur's personal conduct strictly adhered to the code. One friend he had known since their youth in Milwaukee, the sister of General Billy Mitchell, lunched with him at West Point and was surprised at his demeanor, "for he was now quite serious and reserved, no longer gay and full of fun." Major William A. Ganoe attributed this attitude to MacArthur's view of himself as an aristocratic gentleman: "To him the word gentleman held a religious meaning. It was sacredly higher than any act of Congress." [28]

Courtship and Marriage

Although MacArthur usually spent his evenings at home reviewing reports from his subordinates, he occasionally took time to attend social events. The position of superintendent of the academy carried with it considerable prestige, which meant that MacArthur and his mother entertained many distinguished guests on the grounds of West Point. It was at one of these events that Douglas MacArthur met a beautiful, wealthy, and lively woman, twenty-six-year-old Louise Cromwell Brooks, a divorcée with two young children. Pinky did not ap-

When MacArthur returned to West Point as the superintendent, he restored the academic program by enriching the liberal arts curriculum and modernizing the instruction in the sciences.

MacArthur proposed marriage the night that he first met Louise Cromwell Brooks. They married a short time after, on Valentine's Day.

prove of the match, but MacArthur was captivated. He proposed marriage the night he met her. She herself was to recall later that MacArthur was "the handsomest man I ever met." [29]

Theirs was a short courtship. The couple were married on Valentine's Day 1922 at the bride's family mansion in Palm Beach, Florida. Pinky did not attend, claiming poor health. When the couple returned from their honeymoon, she moved back to Washington, D.C., to live with her son Arthur.

Back to the Philippines

MacArthur was soon on the move again as well. Within the year, he received orders to return to the Philippines, to take command of the army's Philippine department. Gossips suggested that Pershing, MacArthur's old adversary, had arranged the faraway post out of spite. Pershing had once courted Louise Brooks himself. The Philippine assignment would maroon the new bride far from the social life of Philadelphia, Washington, D.C., and Palm Beach. Pershing denied the rumors, calling them "poppycock," but the story refused to die.

MacArthur said not a word in complaint about the orders. In fact, he looked forward to going back to the Philippines. His new assignment gave him complete authority and insulated him from the political pressures of Washington. His job was to build up the defenses of the Philippines, so that when the country became independent, it would be able to defend itself. MacArthur believed that the islands were a tempting target for Japan's militarists. He would see that the country was prepared to look after itself.

Family Difficulties

These were unhappy years for Louise MacArthur. She was in love with her husband but not with military life. She found the tropical heat in the Philippines unbearable. She missed her friends. She was often bored, since she had little to keep her occupied.

In 1923, Douglas's brother Arthur, now a highly decorated naval officer for his work developing tactics and strategy in submarine warfare, died unexpectedly, and Douglas MacArthur returned "home," which pleased his mother and wife.

On January 17, 1925, MacArthur received his second star, becoming the youngest major general in the U.S. Army. His command was based in Baltimore, Maryland, where the MacArthurs moved into an elaborate estate owned by Louise. She was much happier now that she could enjoy the local social scene, but friction over MacArthur's chosen career remained. His wife hoped she could persuade MacArthur to take a prestigious position in the private sector and was ready to find that job for him through her family connections. MacArthur, though, was determined to make his career in the army and was not to be persuaded.

The Olympics

It was a difficult time for Douglas MacArthur. The 1920s were bleak years for a professional soldier. Military budgets were meager, and much of his time was spent giving speeches about the importance of being prepared for future wars. He urged college students to join ROTC (the Reserve Officers' Training Corps) and anyone else to take advantage of CMTC (the Citizens' Military Training Corps) programs. These were not challenging assignments; now it was MacArthur's turn to be bored.

In 1927 an unexpected opportunity arose to put his organizational skills to work in the public arena. Just a few months before the 1928 Olympic Games were to take place in the Netherlands, the president of the U.S. Olympic Committee died. The committee needed someone who could take charge of the U.S. team immediately. MacArthur's physical fitness and sports program at West Point was well known to the members of the Olympic Committee, and his organizational skills were unquestioned. The army granted MacArthur a one-year leave of absence.

As the new president of the U.S. Olympic Committee, MacArthur participated in all aspects of training, coaching, and arranging transportation and housing for the athletes during their stay in the Netherlands. The American team did well in competition, and MacArthur shared in the subsequent publicity.

Back in Uniform

Once MacArthur returned to the army, he was again assigned to the Philippines. According to biographer D. Clayton James, "As departmental commander, MacArthur's principal duties were concerned with training, maneuvers, inspections, equipment, and the host of other routine matters that make up the activities of an overseas department during peacetime."[30] This time he made the journey without his wife; the couple had further drifted apart over the years. In June 1929 they were divorced. The failure of his marriage did not hamper his career, however. Within another year he was back in the States with yet another promotion, to three-star, or lieutenant, general.

MacArthur at the Olympics

MacArthur took on the assignment of president of the U.S. Olympic Committee with relish, since it gave him another chance to be in the public eye, as Geoffrey Perret writes in Old Soldiers Never Die.

"The Olympic assignment was made for him, and he reveled in it. He got high on every success, took every defeat to heart. He led the team as it paraded during the opening ceremonies, dined with Queen Wilhemina of Holland and fussed over his athletes like a mother hen. The main thing, though, was to win, to bring back the medals. No one believed in medals more than MacArthur. And when the American boxing team manager withdrew his fighters from the competition in protest after an outrageously bad decision, MacArthur ordered them to fight their remaining bouts. He told them sternly, 'Americans do not quit.' In the end he had the profound satisfaction of seeing the Olympic team he took to Holland dominate the games. It set seven world records and seventeen Olympic records and returned home with twice as many medals as any other nation. He gave each member of the team a gold charm as a token of his appreciation for his or her efforts."

On August 6, 1930, President Herbert Hoover appointed Douglas MacArthur the army chief of staff. By tradition, the position should have gone to an older general of higher rank; at age fifty, MacArthur would be the youngest man ever to hold the post.

In Washington on November 5, 1930, MacArthur was sworn in as chief of staff, an honor that not even his father, a three-star general, had attained. His proud mother pinned the four stars of a full general on his shoulders. Pinky MacArthur, now seventy-eight and very frail, moved with her son into the army's "Number One Quarters"—the chief of staff's large brick home at Fort Myer, across the Potomac River from Washington. Then, as he said later, he got ready to "face the music." Since the end of World War I, the size of the U.S. Army had been greatly reduced. He was the commander of a tiny army in a world of giants. A bill passed by Congress in 1932 reduced the number of regular officers on active duty from twelve thousand to ten thousand, with a corresponding cut in the ranks of enlisted men. In addition, MacArthur soon found himself forced to carry out an ugly task.

The Bonus Army

In his new role as the nation's top army officer, he was forced to comply with an order that proved extremely unpopular with the American public and put him in the position of leading army troops against their own countrymen. Congress had voted to grant a one-thousand-dollar bonus to all World War I veterans, which was to be paid by the year 1945. The nation, however, was in the midst of the Great Depression, and veterans needed the money immediately to pay for food for their families.

In May 1932, seventeen thousand veterans and their families traveled to Washington, D.C., to take part in the so-called Bonus March. They set up tents and cardboard shacks in public parks, on streets, wherever they could find a spot. For the next two months they held parades and rallies, but Congress took no action. Most of the discouraged men went home, but as many as two thousand diehard demonstrators remained. Police units were ordered to demolish the encampment. On July 28 hand-to-hand fighting broke out between the demonstrators and police. Rocks became weapons. Finally the army was called in to restore order.

The army troops resorted to tear gas. Pictures in newspapers of troops battling unarmed civilians who had once fought for their country aroused indignation and outrage among the American public. MacArthur, pictured riding into the melee on a white horse, was blamed for the violence, which left more than a hundred casualties. It was one of the saddest moments of his career. Even though he felt he was not to blame for what happened, he would never forget that day.

The Civilian Conservation Corps

The Bonus Army riot and the concurrent public disillusion over the economic depression helped sweep President Herbert Hoover out of office in the elections of November 1932. Democrat Franklin Delano Roosevelt was elected president on his

Two thousand WWI veterans set up tents and shacks in Washington, D.C., to publicize their demand for the much needed bonus Congress had granted to them. They became known as the Bonus Army.

promise to restore the country's economy by increasing spending on civilian projects. Although Roosevelt and MacArthur respected each other, they would often clash over resulting cuts in the military budget.

Among the president's so-called New Deal programs to help put men back to work was organization of a force to undertake projects of reforestation, flood control, soil rehabilitation, development of national park facilities, and other activities aimed at conserving the nation's resources. On March 21, 1933, the bill to create the Civilian Conservation Corps (CCC) was sent to Congress, where it passed ten days later. In spite of MacArthur's reluctance to have the army involved in the effort, he set about planning for recruitment, training, and logistical support for the CCC. The careful planning paid off: During the first three months of World War I, the War

Department had been able to mobilize 181,000 men. During the period from May 12 through July 1, 1933, the army mobilized 275,000 CCC recruits. Much of the credit went to MacArthur, but the general was looking further from domestic affairs to political developments overseas.

Preparing for the Next War

MacArthur was aware that the Japanese were marching through Manchuria and China and that Italian dictator Benito Mussolini and Germany's chancellor Adolf Hitler were building their war machines in Europe. He felt that it was time to strengthen the armed forces of the United States, not to cut back on training and recruiting. Roosevelt did not agree. The treasury could not fund both his New Deal programs and military buildup.

MacArthur decided that a dramatic gesture was needed, so he went to the White House to argue his case directly, announcing, "If you pursue this policy, Mr. President, you will destroy the American Army. I have no choice but to oppose you publicly. I shall ask for my immediate relief as Chief of Staff, and retirement from the Army. Then I shall take this fight directly to the people!"[31] Saluting, he turned on his heel and left the White House. MacArthur wondered afterward if this had been a foolish act. He had never consid-

---

The Bonus March

MacArthur was well aware of the criticism he received for dispersing the Bonus Marchers. In self-defense, he blamed others for the violence. In his autobiography he quotes from the 1949 testimony of one John Pace before a congressional committee.

"I feel responsible in part for the oft repeated lie about President Hoover and General MacArthur. I led the left wing of the communist section of the bonus march. I was ordered by my Red superiors to provoke riots. I was told to use every trick to bring about bloodshed in the hopes that President Hoover would be forced to call out the army. The communists didn't care how many veterans were killed. I was told Moscow had ordered riots and bloodshed in the hopes that this might set off the revolution. My communist bosses were jumping with joy on July 28 when the Washington police killed one veteran. The Army was called out by President Hoover and didn't fire a shot or kill a man. General MacArthur put down a Moscow directed revolution without bloodshed and that is why the communists hate him."

---

ered going into politics, but it seemed to him nothing less would safeguard national security.

The president reconsidered MacArthur's arguments and was persuaded that the country might indeed be vulnerable militarily. If that were the case, he needed a strong military leader at this precise moment. Roosevelt sent a message to his allies in Congress to stop fighting for cuts in military spending. MacArthur was once more secure in his job.

Roosevelt continued to call on MacArthur for his opinions on civilian as well as military matters. MacArthur ventured to ask one day why the president relied on him in this way. Roosevelt replied, "Douglas, to me you are a symbol of the conscience of America."[32]

MacArthur wanted to be more than just a symbol; he wanted complete control of building up the nation's defenses. Control over the military had always been a civilian responsibility, however, and Roosevelt's advisers felt that MacArthur was overstepping his authority. The problem for MacArthur's opponents was how to ease the general out of his post in a way that would not cause further controversy.

A Question of Titles

On Roosevelt's orders, MacArthur returned to the Philippines to help further strengthen the defenses of that country. Under Roosevelt's plan he would be given the title of high commissioner to the Philippines. This was a hollow honor with little prestige, because the moment he ceased to be chief of staff he reverted to the lower rank of major general. Instead, MacArthur accepted the offer of the Philippine government to become an officer in the Philippine armed forces (while officially attached to the U.S. Army). Manuel Quezon, Philippine president and an old friend of MacArthur, was delighted. In Washington, MacArthur's jubilant enemies congratulated themselves that they had succeeded in sending him into exile.

On October 1, 1935, MacArthur, accompanied by his eighty-two-year-old mother, his widowed sister-in-law, Mary MacCalla MacArthur, and his aides Dwight Eisenhower and Thomas Jefferson Davis, headed for San Francisco to board the ship *President Hoover*, bound for Manila.

Meeting His Future Wife

It was on this voyage that MacArthur met the woman who one day would become his second wife. Thirty-five-year-old Jean Faircloth, from Murfreesboro, Tennessee, was bound for Shanghai. She and MacArthur met at the captain's table the day before the ship put into the port of Honolulu. One story has it that after going ashore the next day, Jean returned to her cabin and found a large bouquet of flowers from MacArthur.

When MacArthur's mother met the young woman, she was delighted. Both women were of southern heritage. Moreover, Jean had inherited a rather substantial estate from her father. She had never been married and enjoyed traveling to exotic places. She had, as MacArthur seems to have realized, almost from the outset, all the makings of a good army wife.

A Son Is Born

MacArthur's pleasure in becoming a father is recorded in D. Clayton James's The Years of MacArthur.

"MacArthur's joy was complete when Jean bore him a son on February 21, 1938. Born at Sternberg Hospital, Manila, the seven-and-one-half-pound baby was named Arthur after his gandfather, uncle, and great grandfather. Appropriately in view of the father's strong sense of family heritage, the infant was baptized on his grandfather's birthday June 2: the Episcopalian ceremony was witnessed by Manuel and Aurora Quezon, who served as godparents. A Chinese woman named Loh Chieu—nicknamed 'Ah Cheu' by the MacArthurs—had been employed in April.

She and Mrs. MacArthur sometimes sided against the general on the treatment of an infant. On one occasion, for instance, the two women had been reading some literature on child psychology and concluded that Arthur was too pampered. So they decided that the next time he started crying, despite good health, a full stomach and dry diapers, they would simply let him lie and wail. On the first such experiment, however, General MacArthur walked in unexpectedly. Seeing his wife and the amah calmly ignoring the child's wailing, he rushed over, tenderly picked him up, and walked him until he had quieted. The psychology books were soon discarded, and the insatiably protective love of the father was allowed to continue in whatever form he chose, to the delight of the general and his son."

MacArthur's second wife Jean gave birth to their son in Manila. They named him Arthur after his grandfather, uncle, and great grandfather.

The Death of Mary MacArthur

Little more than a month after they reached Manila, Pinky died. The loss of his mother was a devastating blow to Douglas MacArthur. As he said, "Of the four of us, who had started out on the plains of New Mexico, three were now gone, leaving me in my loneliness only a memory of the households we had shared, so filled with graciousness and old fashioned living."[33] Much has been said of the influence Pinky had on her son. Her most enduring and important legacy to him was a profoundly emotional nature nourished by a dramatic imagination.

Despite his grief, MacArthur had a job to do. Manuel Quezon appointed MacArthur to the rank of field marshal, a position created especially for MacArthur. He was flattered and wanted to look very grand for the swearing-in ceremony.

He designed an elaborate outfit: black pants and a white tunic covered with medals, stars, and gold cord. A gold-braided cap completed the uniform. Aurora Quezon, the first lady of the Philippines, presented him with a gold baton.

Aside from the pomp and glory of his new position, a lonely life seemed to be ahead for him. He did, however, maintain a correspondence with Jean Faircloth. When in April 1937 he returned to the United States for his mother's burial, he took the time to travel to New York and renew his acquaintance with Jean.

Eighteen months after their first introduction, MacArthur and Jean were married in a brief ceremony before a justice of the peace. The couple then headed for the Waldorf Hotel and a wedding breakfast of

Manuel Quezon, the first president of the Philippines, was chosen by MacArthur and his wife to be their son's godfather.

ham and eggs. Soon after, the couple returned to Manila. On February 21, 1938, their son was born. He was named Arthur in honor of his grandfather and uncle. Manuel Quezon was chosen as his godfather. The family was now complete, but this warm family scene did not distract MacArthur from duties he took very seriously: preparing a defense for the Philippines.

Defending the Philippines

In planning a defensive strategy for the Philippines, MacArthur faced a daunting task. The Philippine archipelago contains some seven thousand islands, spanning sixteen degrees of latitude. U.S. Navy strategists believed that it would be almost impossible to hold the islands if they were attacked. Moreover, they argued, Manila Bay had almost no strategic value. In his plan, MacArthur played down the role of naval vessels and pointed out that the rugged terrain of the Philippines, with its mountains and jungles, would hamper invaders. He drew up a plan that provided for a force of 920 officers and 10,000 enlisted men—less than a full division of troops. This tiny army would in turn train an additional 40,000 young men, aged eighteen to twenty-two. He begged the U.S. Congress for money to equip a Philippine army, but he had few supporters at home. Let the Filipinos take care of themselves, was the prevalent attitude.

MacArthur was passionate in defending what he sometimes called "my second country." This passion led to clashes with the heads of all branches of the U.S. armed forces, which led to his being called back to the States in the spring of 1941. MacArthur was furious and responded by resigning from the army. Although his decision was accepted with "deep regret," MacArthur's service to his country and to the Philippines was not finished, as events would soon prove.

Chapter

5 World War II

On July 26, 1941, MacArthur was called back to active duty as commanding general of U.S. Army forces in the Far East. By the middle of 1941, observers in the United States were beginning to believe his warnings about Japanese aggression. The United States finally began to send shiploads of supplies to the Philippines. MacArthur prepared his troops to dig in and defend the shoreline around Manila Bay. MacArthur made one mistake, though. The full force of war would come from the skies, not from the sea.

On December 7, 1941, airplanes launched from Japanese aircraft carriers attacked the U.S. naval fleet at Pearl Harbor, Hawaii. The attack was a complete disaster for the United States. More than 2,300 Americans were killed, another 1,100 wounded. Nineteen U.S. Navy ships were sunk or severely damaged; nearly 200 of the army's airplanes were destroyed by attacks on nearby Hickam Field.

Almost simultaneously other Japanese planes attacked Hong Kong, Thailand, Guam, and Wake Island. On December 8 it was the Philippines' turn.

The first hours of the conflict in the Philippines were filled with confusion. At 12:35 P.M. Japanese planes swooped in and destroyed every American B-17 at Clark airfield, north of Manila. As the bombs ex-

ploded on the runways, a message arrived at MacArthur's command headquarters declaring a state of war. It was a message from the Japanese that had been decoded by the communication office. "Very interesting and timely,"[34] was MacArthur's sarcastic reply. The quick success of the Japanese quickly broke MacArthur's basic plan to hold them off at the beaches. The poorly trained and poorly equipped Filipino forces crumbled.

MacArthur's plan had been to hold Manila until fresh supplies could be shipped into the Philippines from the United States. The plan, however, was doomed by the success of the attack at Pearl Harbor; the heavy losses the Pacific fleet had suffered ruled out any rescue mission. Moreover, strategists gave the war in Europe priority, and no ships from the Atlantic fleet could be spared to keep the supply lines open in the Far East.

Within a month the Japanese landed two large armies on the Philippine island of Luzon. Their plan was to attack from two directions in order to trap MacArthur's troops on the broad, flat plain around Manila. MacArthur evaded the trap by evacuating his troops to the rugged highlands of the Bataan Peninsula, which formed one side of Manila Bay, while fighting a rearguard action. He declared Manila an open

MacArthur was called back to active duty in 1941 to help counter the threat of Japanese aggression. That threat became reality when the Japanese bombed Pearl Harbor (pictured).

city, which by all the rules of modern warfare meant that it would not be defended and therefore should not be bombed. The invaders, however, devastated the city, and inhabitants who thought that they would be safe were taken prisoner.

Corregidor

Meanwhile, MacArthur, his wife, his son, and his staff moved to the fortress of Corregidor, which offered some protection from bombing attacks. Corregidor is a volcanic island about twenty-two square miles in area, two miles from Bataan, thirty miles from Manila. The fortress was built on solid rock, and its fortifications were of reinforced concrete. In spite of the strong walls of the fort, however, the one-hundred-foot-long tunnel under the fortress, dug out of rock fifty years before, was the only safe place to be during air raids. Unfortunately, not all of Corregidor's nine thousand civilians and military personnel could be housed there. Defensive dugouts were scattered around the rest of the island.

The days that followed the retreat to Corregidor brought out both the attractive and less attractive aspects of MacArthur's character. He was truly dedicated to the fighting force he was directing, but at this crucial moment in history he was also dickering with President Quezon to rehire him as Philippine field marshal to bolster his own career. MacArthur ordered reserves of food, what little there was, to be transferred from the mainland to Corregidor. The forces on Bataan had to fend for themselves. Only once did he visit the troops on Bataan, which were only three miles away, five minutes by torpedo boat.

Because of his perceived callousness toward the troops who were starving within sight of the fortifications of Corregidor, MacArthur earned the title "Dugout Doug." Even so, MacArthur showed little concern for his own safety during air raids. While others hunkered down to avoid the bomb blasts, the general frequently sauntered to the opening of the tunnel to observe how many planes were attacking and what type of ammunition they were using.

Defeat

MacArthur would not admit to others that he saw defeat looming, but he considered it most likely that the war for the Philippines

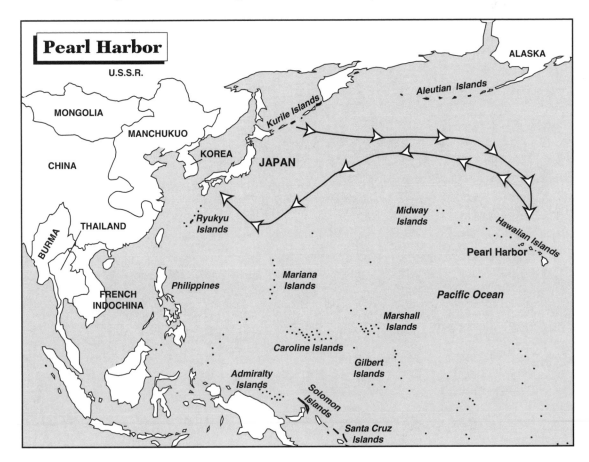

Pearl Harbor

U.S.S.R.
ALASKA
MONGOLIA
Aleutian Islands
MANCHUKUO
Kurile Islands
KOREA
JAPAN
CHINA
Midway Islands
Ryukyu Islands
Hawaiian Islands
THAILAND
Pearl Harbor
BURMA
Mariana Islands
Philippines
Pacific Ocean
FRENCH INDOCHINA
Marshall Islands
Caroline Islands
Gilbert Islands
Admiralty Islands
Solomon Islands
Santa Cruz Islands

could not be won. The fighting on Bataan was fierce and constant. With no replacements available, the roster of soldiers who could be considered on active duty was dwindling alarmingly. He would be a prime target for capture, but MacArthur did not wish to sully his reputation by being paraded as a prisoner. He determined that he would end his own life before he would let that happen.

MacArthur had to consider his family, however. He urged General George Marshall to provide a submarine transport for his wife and son, but Jean would not think of such a move. The submarine left with Manuel Quezon, his wife, and a few other top officials of the Philippines government.

On February 23, Douglas MacArthur received orders to travel to Mindanao, one of the southernmost Philippines islands. From there he was to proceed to Melbourne, Australia. General Jonathan Wainwright was to command the ragged forces left behind. MacArthur protested that this

American survivors of Bataan and Corregidor. Many men perished from disease, injury, starvation, and enemy brutality.

Leadership by Example

MacArthur describes life during the bombing of Corregidor in his autobiography, Reminiscences.

"My new headquarters was located in an area of the Malinta Tunnel. Carved deep in the rock, the central tunnel was actually the terminal point of a streetcar line. Other passages had been hewn out of the rock and these housed hospital wards, storerooms, and ammunition magazines. The headquarters were bare, glaringly lighted, and contained only the essential furniture and equipment for administrative procedure. At the sound of the air alarm, an aide and I would make our way out through the crowded civilians seeking shelter in the main passageway, huddled silently in that hunched down, age-old Oriental squat of patience and stolid resignation, onto the highway to watch the weaving pattern of the enemy's formations.

There was nothing of bravado in this. It was simply my duty. The gunners at the batteries, the men in the fox holes, they too were in the open. They liked to see me with them at such moments. The subtle corrosion of panic and fatigue, or the feeling of just being fed up, can be arrested by the intervention of the leaders."

move would be a fatal blow to the morale of the troops; he compared it to a captain leaving his sinking ship.

After two more messages directly from President Roosevelt, telling him that his presence was needed in Australia, MacArthur agreed to make plans for departure. On March 1 he ordered the four remaining P-40 planes to circle Manila Bay to discourage a Japanese air attack. Seventeen crewmen of the four PT-41 torpedo boats were put on standby for a secret mission. The sailors thought they might be bound for China. Instead they picked up the general, Jean, little Arthur, and his nurse. Other passengers included thirteen army officers, two naval officers, and a staff sergeant technician.

A Narrow Escape

The tiny convoy crept through the minefields of Manila Bay. Twice they came close to enemy vessels but slipped by unnoticed. Although the boats had been built for speed, they had not been equipped with spare parts, and two of them never made it to the rendezvous. It was a rough ride;

both Douglas and Jean MacArthur suffered seasickness, but by the time they had arrived at their destination, the general was standing on the prow as if he had spent his life at sea.

Even after the boats reached Mindanao, the danger was not over. MacArthur and his party were still on Philippine soil, and capture by the enemy was a possibility. Four days elapsed before they continued on their way; MacArthur refused to board the first dangerously decrepit aircraft available and radioed for another plane.

Even though a more reliable airplane was eventually found, the danger was not over. They had almost reached Darwin when they were turned away because an enemy raid was in progress. Instead, they were diverted to an emergency airfield about fifty miles away. Yet another airplane flight and a thousand-mile train trip lay ahead, but at last the MacArthurs were safe.

At a stop in Adelaide, MacArthur learned by wire that he had been awarded the coveted Medal of Honor. Now he could wear on his chest the highest of all American honors. Arthur MacArthur and Douglas MacArthur had become the

first father and son—and the only such pair since—to win the Medal of Honor.

Command Post

MacArthur soon found that he would be commanding very little in the way of a fighting force. The army that he thought awaited him did not exist. Vice Admiral Herbert Leary's naval forces had been destroyed in the Battle of the Java Sea. Fewer than a hundred airplanes were serviceable, including obsolete Australian Gypsy Moths with engines that had to be started by spinning the propellers by hand. There were no tanks. The situation was desperate and would be for some time to come.

MacArthur was not at a loss for words. When reporters urged him to comment, he wrote his words on the back of an envelope: "The President of the United States ordered me to break through the Japanese lines . . . for the purpose, as I understand it, of organizing the American offensive against Japan, a primary object of which is the relief of the Philippines. I came through and I will return."[35]

The Fall of Corregidor

Before leaving Corregidor, MacArthur had divided the Philippines into four commands, with General Wainwright responsible only for those troops on the island of Luzon, so that when the inevitable Japanese takeover occurred, Wainwright would be able to surrender only part of the forces in the Philippines. What MacArthur hated to admit was that there would be no troops to surrender if food supplies did not arrive soon. Those who had survived the fighting were now starving to death.

On April 3 Japanese general Masaharu Homma launched a fierce attack on the southern part of Luzon. Homma expected to have to fight his way through three lines of defenses. There was only one, and that line was broken on April 7. With the Japanese attack, Bataan fell. Now the only American troops guarding the harbor were those holed up on Corregidor.

For twenty-seven days Corregidor was bombarded, and on May 5 Japanese forces landed. The 4th Marine Regiment virtually wiped out the first wave of attackers, but the second came ashore with light tanks. The thought of high explosive shells penetrating

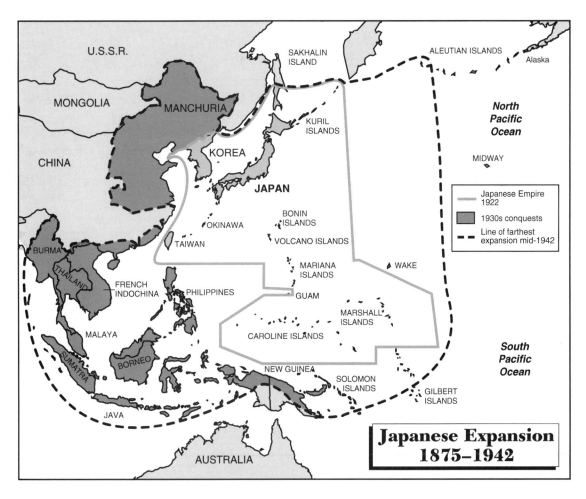

Japanese Expansion 1875–1942

the mouth of the tunnel, in which a thousand wounded soldiers were crammed, was more than Wainwright could bear. On May 6 the American flag was lowered.

Homma ordered Wainwright to surrender the American forces elsewhere in the Philippines. Wainwright countered with the argument that the rest of the forces were under the command of General MacArthur. Homma produced copies of intercepted messages from Washington addressing Wainwright as commander in chief. No such word had reached his headquarters, but with no other alternative, he ordered the surrender of all remaining American and Filipino troops in the islands. Wainwright radioed Roosevelt that he would have to surrender "with broken heart, but not in shame." [36]

The Japanese next forced their prisoners on Bataan and Corregidor on a brutal death march across the hot, dusty plains of Luzon. This surrender was America's largest ever, this defeat the U.S. Army's worst ever. Arguments between MacArthur and his superiors about who was responsible for the defeat began immediately. MacArthur blamed General Marshall for the surrender

Farewell to Corregidor

One American eyewitness to Mac-Arthur's farewell to the Philippines has been quoted in the book Banners and the Glory *by the editors of the* Army Times.

"Corregidor rises abruptly from the water's edge where Lieutenant Bulkey's PT stood by. All boarded promptly except the General, who stopped and turned slowly to look back. What a transformation had taken place in that normally beautiful spot. Its green foliage was gone and with its trees, its shrubs, its flowers, all bruised and torn by the hail of relentless bombardment. That warped and twisted face of scorched rock seemed to reflect the writhings of a tortured body. It had become a black mass of destruction.

What thoughts must have crowded his mind as he looked his farewell. And then I saw him slowly raise his cap in salute, there in the twighlight, as he glanced up through the smoky haze with its smell of death and stench of destruction thick in the night air. And it seemed to me that I could see a sudden convulsive twitch in the muscles of his jaw, a sudden whitening in the bronze of his face. I said to the man next to me, 'What's his chance of getting through?'

'About one in five,' was the reply."

After the surrender of troops in the Pacific, Mac-Arthur was to share power with Admiral Nimitz, an order he strongly opposed.

because he had given Wainwright the command of all troops. Marshall answered by saying it was impossible for MacArthur to evaluate conditions three thousand miles away in Australia.

MacArthur countered with even more criticism of war planning in Washington. He felt that too much emphasis was being placed on the war in Europe. Troops and equipment were being funneled there, leaving the war in the Pacific a mere sideshow. MacArthur was also critical of the military leadership in Europe. He called Eisenhower, the commander in Europe, a desk soldier.

MacArthur had flown to Australia thinking he would command America's Pacific war against Japan. Instead, President Roosevelt ordered that a dual command be set up. The war at sea was to be commanded by Admiral Chester Nimitz, chief of the Pacific fleet. MacArthur was to direct the land war. He was being ordered to share power, something he would not do without debate.

Chapter

6 "I Shall Return"

Refusing to accept defeat, MacArthur wrote home to a friend, "To make something out of nothing seems to be my military fate in the twilight of my service. I have led one lost cause and am trying desperately not to have it two."[37] Then a bull-necked, energetic, cursing, fifty-one-year-old general, George C. Kenney, arrived on the scene and somehow put together the pieces of the dilapidated Allied air forces. In addition to reinvigorating the Allies' efforts to fight a war in the air, his arrival seemed to give MacArthur new spirit.

Instead of concentrating on defending Australia, MacArthur sought to bring the front closer to the Japanese. He proposed to move troops north from Australia to the nearby island of New Guinea to stop the Japanese before they could get near Australia. This would save Australia from invasion and give MacArthur an opportunity to go on the offensive.

As he outlined his strategy he pointed to the charts in front of him: "We'll fight them where they ain't . . . ," he said. "They won't expect us. Their small army will be easily beaten. Our losses will not be great. We'll build air bases and move forward. We won't fight where the Japanese are strong. We'll leap over the top of them and cut off their supplies. They'll starve."[38]

The arrival of General George C. Kenney reinvigorated the Allies' efforts to fight a war in the air and brought MacArthur renewed spirits.

His leapfrogging tactics proved successful, but any hope that the going would be easy was dashed. One of the bloodiest battles on New Guinea was fought at the tiny plantation settlement of Buna on the northern coast of the island. General Robert Eichelberger was the man in charge. His orders from MacArthur were plain: "Bob, I want you to take Buna, or not come back alive." [MacArthur] paused for a moment, and then pointed a finger, "And that goes for your chief of staff, too. Do you understand?"[39]

The order was carried out, but not without heavy casualties. The battle that included Buna, Gona, and Sanananda resulted in nearly nine thousand men killed or wounded.

Working together over the next seven months, the army, navy, and marines recaptured the Gilbert Islands, the Marshall Islands, and Saipan. The plan was always the same. American battleships would bombard lightly held enemy islands. Then the Japanese garrison would be assaulted by troops ferried ashore on flat-bottomed landing craft. The theory was that by cutting off the Japanese supply lines, their forces would starve, or as Admiral William Halsey would later put it, "wither on the vine."

By 1944, MacArthur's strategy of island hopping had proven successful. He wanted to continue the momentum of attack and head on to the Philippines, but as he was planning this great offensive, he received coded orders to fly to Hawaii to discuss military strategy with "Mr. Big." MacArthur suspected that "Mr. Big" was President Roosevelt, so he saw the meeting as an opportunity to present his plan to head directly to the Philippines to the commander in chief personally.

The meeting took place on July 26, 1944, aboard the battleship *Baltimore;* MacArthur arranged to make a theatrical entrance. Admirals Nimitz and Halsey had already arrived. Roosevelt was seated in his chair. All were waiting when with a wail of a siren, traffic was cleared and an open black limousine screeched to a stop at the dock. MacArthur emerged in leisurely fashion and strode up the gangplank, wearing his now famous floppy hat and a leather jacket.

"Hello Doug," the president said, a seasoned performer himself, sensing that he had lost the spotlight. "What are you doing with that leather jacket on—it's darn hot today."

"Well, I've just landed from Australia. It's pretty cold down there."[40]

The agenda was to determine the strategy for the final assault on Japan. Nimitz was the first to speak. He outlined the navy's plan for a landing on Formosa; this would be the base for the attack on Japan.

Then it was MacArthur's turn to press his case for liberating the Philippines first: "Mr. President . . . the nation will never forgive you if you approve a plan which leaves 17 million Christian American subjects to wither in the Philippines under the conqueror's heel until the peace treaty frees them. You might do it for reasons of strategy or tactics, but politically it would ruin you."[41]

Roosevelt was undecided. He was facing another election, so public opinion would be important. He also had to deal with the war in Europe, which was nearing a crucial stage.

MacArthur's Tactics Win the Day

During the summer and fall of 1944, the president's attention was focused on Europe, where Allied forces were closing in

Truman's Thoughts About MacArthur

President Harry S. Truman's dislike for MacArthur is well documented. Geoffrey Perret, in his book Old Soldiers Never Die, *quotes various entries in Truman's diary.*

"As the President turned his mind to what he should do with Japan once the Emperor had surrendered, he raged at the thought of having to deal with "Mr. Prima Donna, Brass Hat, Five Star MacArthur (sic). He's worse than the Cabots and Lodges. They at least talked to one another before they told God what to do. Mc tells God what to do right off. It is a very great pity we have to have stuffed shirts like that in key positions. I don't see why in hell Roosevelt didn't order Wainwright home and let MacArthur be the martyr. . . . We'd have a real general and a fighting man if we had Wainwright and not a play actor and a bunco man such as we have now."

President Truman's opinion of Mac-Arthur was one of contempt.

on Germany. Many of Roosevelt's advisers felt that only after the Allies defeated Germany should attention be turned to the war in the Pacific.

MacArthur refused to wait and drew up his own plan for invading the Philippines. He had convinced Halsey and Nimitz that a direct assault on Tokyo would stretch supply lines too far, and that his plan was thus safer for Allied troops. First, he would land on one of the smaller islands, Leyte, in October 1944. From there he would strike the island of Mindanao and finally Luzon, where the Philippine capital of Manila is located.

On October 14, 15, and 16 of 1944, a convoy with seventy-four thousand troops headed from New Guinea toward Leyte. MacArthur was aboard the cruiser *Nashville,* his cabin decorated with the framed photos of his family that he always carried with him. He was dressed in khaki trousers and an open shirt, the four stars on his collar the only concession to rank. He was ready for his dramatic return.

The navy's big guns thundered a salvo toward the beaches of Leyte. Through the smoke and haze MacArthur could recognize the docks of Tacloban, where he had stepped ashore forty years before on his first tour of duty as a young lieutenant fresh out of West Point.

The Japanese knew that they must prevent the Americans from making Leyte the base of operations if they were to hold the Philippines. Soon they were funneling everything they had—planes, troops, and navy—into the defense of Leyte.

MacArthur, watching from the deck of the *Nashville,* announced that he would be riding onto the beach with the third wave of troops. With him was the new Philippine president, Sergio Aosmena. It seemed only proper that the head of state of the Philippines and MacArthur, the returning hero, should land on Philippine soil together.

"I Have Returned"

The launch carrying the general and President Aosmena swerved toward shore through the smoke and din of the ongoing battle. Some fifty feet from shore the boat hit a sandbar and went aground. MacArthur was the first to step out of the boat into knee-deep water. A combat photographer was there to record the dramatic moment.

MacArthur strode directly toward the front line, corncob pipe in his teeth. Rain dampened his uniform as he addressed all who could hear: "People of the Philippines, I have returned. By the grace of Almighty God our forces stand again on Philippine soil."[42] The American and Philippine flags were hoisted over Philippine soil for the first time since they had been lowered over Corregidor almost three years before. The Allied forces had successfully established a beachhead from which they could push on toward Manila and, ultimately, Tokyo.

Five Stars

Just before Christmas 1944, President Roosevelt promoted MacArthur to the newly created rank of general of the army, signified by an unprecedented fifth star. Six others received the same honor: Generals George Marshall, Dwight Eisenhower, and Hap Arnold, and Admirals Ernest King,

While storming the beach of Leyte, MacArthur's boat hit a sandbar. The general was the first to step out of the boat and walk to the front line.

William Leahy, and Chester Nimitz. Mac-Arthur, however, let everyone know that he considered himself to outrank them all because he had held the rank of four-star general the longest.

Turner Catledge of the *New York Times* was at the award ceremony and heard MacArthur recall his own exploits. The new five-star general was clearly pleased with himself: "As he spoke, he was variously the military expert, the political figure, the man of destiny . . . we had never met a more egotistical man, no man more aware of his egotism, and more able and determined to back it up with his deeds."[43]

Perhaps MacArthur had a right to boast; just a year before his troops had been pinned down on the island of New Guinea. Now they were nearing their main objective, retaking the island of Luzon. Now nearly a thousand ships carried the largest invasion force ever assembled in the Pacific.

On January 9, 1945, the armada was ready for the assault on Luzon. Again MacArthur planned his grand entrance, a replay of the pictures taken at Leyte. He waded through the surf, the photographers' cameras clicking. Within twelve days the Allied forces had pushed to within twenty miles of Manila. By February 3 all resistance within the city had ended; Manila was in the hands of the Allies. An assault on Corregidor, however, was still going to be necessary.

Paratroopers dropped onto the island fortress as marines came ashore from landing craft. For ten days the Allied troops battled the defenders. Finally on March 1, the last of the Japanese resistance ended. The following day MacArthur boarded a PT boat to officially take command of the fortress he had left three years earlier. He ordered the commander of the invasion force to raise the American flag: "Have your troops hoist the colors to its peak and let no enemy ever haul them down."[44]

While the remnants of Japanese forces in the Philippines were gradually overcome, MacArthur was busy preparing for an assault on Japan, set for October 1945. The war in Europe had ended with Germany's surrender in May; thus, troops were now available for action in the Pacific. MacArthur believed he would be leading his troops to Tokyo itself. Only one thing was to stop him. MacArthur received a visit from Brigadier General Thomas Farrell, with a message directly from Washington. Farrell was granted a fifteen-minute interview. As Farrell later reported:

The General talked for the first thirteen minutes. And, believe me it was fascinating. It was a rundown on what

With the largest invasion force ever assembled in the Pacific, a thousand Allied ships head for the island of Luzon.

The development of the atomic bomb was the deciding factor of the war. After the bomb was dropped on Nagasaki, Emperor Hirohito ordered his forces to surrender.

it might be like when he invaded. Then he looked at his watch and asked me why I was there. I swallowed and told him we had developed the atomic bomb, and would he please keep all of his planes out of the general area of Hiroshima around the end of the first week in August.[45]

Forty-eight hours after MacArthur was informed of the new weapon, the world's first atomic bomb was dropped on Hiroshima. The date was August 6, 1945. Over seventy-eight thousand Japanese men, wo-men, and children were killed, with another forty-eight thousand injured or missing. On August 9 a second A-bomb was dropped on Nagasaki, leaving another seventy-four thousand dead. The next day Japanese emperor Hirohito ordered the Japanese surrender. President Harry S. Truman broadcast his acceptance of the unconditional surrender of Japan, and announced that Britain, China, and Russia had agreed to the appointment of Mac-Arthur as supreme commander of the Allied powers.

7 Surrender

Two days before the official signing of the surrender documents, MacArthur's plane landed at the Atsugi airport, which had once been a base for Japan's feared kamikaze pilots. A thousand U.S. paratroopers had landed just hours earlier to secure the territory for the Allies. The Americans were literally surrounded by 2.5 million Japanese troops, who were still armed. Many experts had predicted guerrilla war when the Americans landed in Japan, but MacArthur made his entrance with only a small contingent of U.S. military for support.

As the official motorcade wound through Yokohama, thirty thousand Japanese troops, with rifles in hand, lined the route. The

The Japanese used tactics such as kamikaze attacks during the war.

Americans were puzzled that the troops faced away from the passing cars. Later this was explained as a sign of honor. The Japanese were not permitted to gaze on their emperor and MacArthur was being shown the same respect. These same troops had also been ordered by their commander to shoot any of their countrymen who tried to sabotage the procession. There was no violence, much to the relief of everyone, and the surrender went forward as scheduled.

At nine o'clock on the morning of September 2, 1945, aboard the battleship *Missouri,* the surrender ceremony opened with a prayer and the playing of "The Star Spangled Banner." Then MacArthur, representing the Allies, approached the microphone:

> We are gathered here, representatives of the major warring powers, to conclude a solemn agreement whereby peace may be restored. . . . It is my earnest hope and indeed the hope of all mankind that from this solemn occasion a better world shall emerge out of the blood and carnage of the past—a world founded upon faith and understanding—a world dedicated to the dignity of man and the fulfillment of his most cherished wish—for freedom, tolerance, and justice. . . . I now invite the representatives of the Emperor of Japan and the Japanese government and the Japanese Imperial Staff Headquarters to sign the instrument of surrender at the place indicated.[46]

On the table rested two copies of the peace treaty, one for the Americans, the other for the Japanese. Once the representatives of Japan had signed the document, MacArthur took five pens from his pocket. Using each in turn, he wrote his name. He handed the first pen to General Wainwright. The second went to Britain's Gen-

General MacArthur signs Japan's surrender documents aboard the USS Missouri.

eral A. S. Percival. The third went to West Point and the fourth to the Naval Academy. A fifth pen would be Jean's. MacArthur's concluding words were simple: "These proceedings are now closed."[47] It had been three years, eight months, and twenty-two days since the bombing of Pearl Harbor. MacArthur had finished one job, and another was just beginning.

Bringing Peace to Japan

MacArthur's first job was to disarm Japan. Ten thousand planes, three thousand tanks, ninety thousand field guns, 3 million small arms, and a million tons of explosives were destroyed and thrown into the sea. Some 6 million Japanese soldiers and sailors were returned to Japan from all over Asia. A million slave laborers, most of them from Korea, China, and Okinawa, and thousands of prisoners of war were returned to their homelands.

Another major task for MacArthur was preparing a new Japanese constitution. He wanted the new constitution to move Japan from its feudal past into a democratic future. Although MacArthur's power to dictate the new constitution was absolute, he wanted the Japanese to write the document themselves. As General Courtney Whitney described it years later: "MacArthur steered his course between letting the Japanese do it, and not letting the Japanese get away with it."[48]

The resulting document removed all political power from the emperor, setting up a constitutional monarchy to serve as the symbol of the state and unity of the people. It created a popularly elected legislature (Diet) vested as the highest organ of state power. Following the American model, the Japanese constitution created separate executive, legislative, and judicial branches of the government.

Japan's first postwar election was held on April 10, 1946, less than a year after the end of the war, and represented a break with the past. Some 13 million women went to the polls for the first time in Japan's history. The old Japanese legislature had comprised lawyers, industrialists, and professional politicians; most of the new Diet was composed of educators, authors, physicians, and farmers. In another change from the past, thirty-eight women were elected to office.

MacArthur oversaw other expansions of Japanese civil and political rights. All political prisoners were released. The dreaded secret police were disbanded. The government was decentralized with local offices created through a modern civil service system so that competent employees could be chosen to serve and be trained in specific jobs. Social security laws were passed, which meant that Japanese people would have ready access to health care. Other legislation encouraged the creation of labor unions, and protected unions from interference from employers, and reformed the education system, making public education possible for those who before had not been able to pay for schooling. New textbooks written by Japanese scholars revised inaccurate accounts of Japanese history.

At MacArthur's insistence, the power of the emperor was eliminated. Hirohito himself read a proclamation that was broadcast to the nation. He admitted that he was not divine and never had been, despite Shinto teaching that all Japanese emperors were descended from gods. "The ties

Under Japan's new constitution, over 13 million women were allowed to vote for the first time in 1946 (right). Although the power of the emperor was eliminated, MacArthur left Hirohito (bottom) in that position as a figurehead.

between us and our people do not depend upon mere legend and myths," he asserted. "They are not predicated on the false concept that the emperor is divine and that the Japanese people are superior to other races and fated to rule the world."[49] The voice was Hirohito's, but the words were Douglas MacArthur's.

MacArthur was heavily criticized for allowing Hirohito to remain as emperor instead of trying him as a war criminal. His reasoning was practical: "We need him as a figurehead. He's still the spiritual leader of Shintoism. By using him on our side, we can get by with an occupation army of only two hundred thousand men. Without him, we would need two million."[50]

Not all Japanese were left unpunished. Among those tried, found guilty, and hanged as war criminals were Generals Tomoyuki Yamashita, the Japanese commander in the Philippines, and Masaharu Homma, who had ordered the Bataan death march.

Outlawing War

It would seem obvious that the victorious Allies would insist that the new Japanese constitution have a nonaggression clause. In fact, such a clause was insisted on by Dr. Joli Matsumoto himself, who would eventually be elected prime minister. He wished to prohibit any military establishment whatsoever, so that all national resources would be devoted to rebuilding Japan's shattered economy.

MacArthur agreed. He confided that he thought that war should be abolished as an outmoded means of resolving disputes

between all nations. After seeing the results of the atom bomb, MacArthur believed this step was inevitable.

Politics at Home

With the successful conclusion of the war, MacArthur was a man in the news. He was a forceful speaker, and many Americans assumed he intended to make a run for the presidency. Indeed, MacArthur had been assured by former president Herbert Hoover of the support of conservative Republicans. Hoover asked MacArthur to declare his intentions and to give Republican leaders an idea of what policies he would propose if he chose to run.

Dealing with the Emperor

Political chronicler John Gunther commends MacArthur for his diplomacy in relations with the Japanese emperor immediately following the Japanese surrender in his book The Riddle of MacArthur.

"In September 1945, immediately after the surrender, people thought that MacArthur would summon the Emperor to him forthwith. There was, in fact, a good deal of pressure on the Supreme Commander, suggesting that he should at once lay down the law to Hirohito and put him in his place. MacArthur did nothing of the kind. He was much more subtle. He knew that, sooner or later, the Emperor was bound to come to him of his own volition, because, as he himself told us, Hirohito would be too curious about his new power to stay away. Also a gentleman with high regard for good blood and breeding, MacArthur did not want to humiliate Hirohito wantonly in the hour of his defeat. Finally, he thought that if he took too severe a line against him or behaved rudely, this might serve to martyrize him in the eyes of his prostrate people."

On March 9, 1948, MacArthur issued a statement that in effect said he would not actively seek the presidency but would accept it if offered. Meanwhile, Dwight Eisenhower was also being considered as a presidential candidate. Eisenhower declined to run, saying that he did not think a life-long professional soldier would make a good presidential candidate. Eisenhower's withdrawal caused MacArthur to change his mind about running. In the 1948 Republican primary in Wisconsin, however, MacArthur came in second, and he fared even worse in subsequent primaries. Governor Thomas Dewey of New York was the eventual Republican nominee. In the general election that November, Democrat Harry Truman was reelected president. MacArthur swore he would never again submit himself to a popular vote.

Vicky. By permission of the *London Evening Standard.*

MacArthur and Eisenhower as Political Strategists

Richard Nixon, Eisenhower's running mate, had an excellent opportunity to observe both MacArthur's and Eisenhower's political strategies. In his book Leaders *he assesses their flaws.*

"FDR once said to MacArthur, 'Douglas, I think you are the best general, but I believe you would be our worst politician.' He was right. MacArthur was not a good politician, and eventually he realized it. His greatest political miscalculation, in fact, was to appear to be interested in politics at all, to attempt personally to convert his enormous prestige into political capital. He should have left the active politicking to those who were willing to act on his behalf.

I believe that Eisenhower wanted to be President as much as MacArthur did, but he was clever enough not to admit it. Though Eisenhower always insisted that he was just an amateur politician, he was in fact a masterly political operator. He instinctively knew that the best way to get the prize was to appear not to be seeking it."

Politics on the Other Side of the World

With his unsuccessful candidacy behind him, MacArthur turned his attention to making Japan a strong and active ally in containing the expansion of Soviet influence in Asia. MacArthur thought his effort was succeeding until early on the morning of June 25, 1950. MacArthur was aroused from his sleep at the American embassy by a telephone call informing him that the North Koreans had attacked South Korea in strength across the 38th parallel, the border between the two nations.

Chapter

8 Korea

As soon as the news of the North Korean invasion reached him, MacArthur ordered all available military equipment rushed to South Korea, but this was little help. The

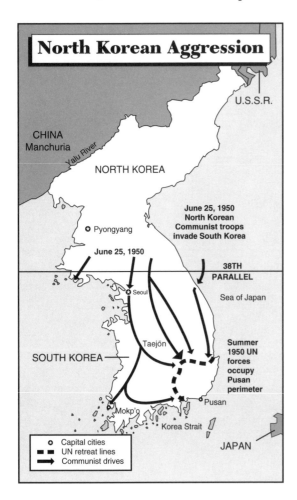

North Korean Aggression

CHINA
Manchuria

Yalu River

NORTH KOREA

U.S.S.R.

⊙ Pyongyang

June 25, 1950
North Korean
Communist troops
invade South Korea

June 25, 1950

38TH
PARALLEL

⊙ Seoul

Sea of Japan

Taejŏn

SOUTH KOREA

Summer
1950 UN
forces
occupy
Pusan
perimeter

Mokp'o

Pusan

Korea Strait

JAPAN

⊙ Capital cities
■ ■ UN retreat lines
➡ Communist drives

troop strength in the Far East had been cut considerably in the four years since World War II had ended. Those still under MacArthur's command had not been trained for combat. There was little to be done, but what MacArthur could do, he decided, was to see for himself just how serious the situation was.

On June 29 MacArthur prepared to board his plane, christened *Bataan,* for a flight to Korea. Just as he was about to enter the plane, a command car came speeding across the airfield. Lieutenant General George E. Stratemeyer, commander of the Far East air force, hoped to persuade him to stay where he was because there was no safe place to land in Korea. MacArthur was not persuaded:

"If I don't go, you'd go yourself, George, wouldn't you?"

"Yes, but I don't count. You're a different matter."

"We go," commanded MacArthur.[51]

When his plane touched down on the bomb-pocked Suwan airfield, he immediately ordered a jeep to take him to the front. It was slow going; the roads were jammed with refugees fleeing the burning city of Seoul. Planes with Russian markings roared overhead at treetop level. MacArthur stood in the middle of the road watching through binoculars as an advancing

The Division of Korea

At the end of World War II, Korea was split in two. Geoffrey Perret explains the rationale of partition in Old Soldiers Never Die.

"When the war ended, two Army colonels named Dean Rush and Charles Bonesteel were entrusted with organizing surrender arrangements in Korea, which had been occupied, looted and raped by the Japanese for nearly fifty years. Purely for the sake of convenience, they decided to have all the Japanese forces north of the thirty-eighth parallel surrender to the Soviets and all Japanese forces south of the parallel surrender to the Americans.

It was optimistically assumed that all Korea would be united in a couple of years under a democratically elected government. That did not happen. Under the Japanese there had been no free Koreans. By 1948 there were exactly two leaders. One was the elderly Bible-thumping Syngman Rhee, who ran a right-wing police state under American protection; the other was Kim II Sung, a vainglorious thug who ran a Communist prison camp under Stalin guidance."

group of North Korean tanks cut through barriers set up hastily by the South Korean forces. Reports reaching MacArthur indicated that at least half of the South Korean army had already been captured or was on the casualty list.

When he returned to Tokyo, MacArthur sent an urgent message to President Truman warning that the retreat of the South Korean army was in fact a disastrous rout. If the invasion was left unchecked, he said, there would be a serious communist threat to both the Philippines and to Japan.

MacArthur was uncertain of Russia's motives in this attack; he felt that Russia might be trying to lure the United States into war with North Korea, which might

eventually lead to war with the huge Chinese forces waiting to the north. By involving its two main adversaries in a protracted conflict, perhaps Russia hoped to be left free to carve up Europe for itself.

Truman was not ready to commit the United States to another devastating war far from its own borders. All he could hope for without bringing about a full-scale war was to slow down the Russian/North Korean advance. He ordered a small number of American troops from Japan to try to stabilize the situation.

MacArthur disagreed with Truman's strategy. "It's Bataan and Corregidor all over again," MacArthur said. "I'm supposed to hold the enemy with a handful of untrained troops, sacrificing lives for time, for the help that never comes!"[52]

A bold plan was needed to create as much havoc among the enemy as possible with a limited number of troops. MacArthur came up with the idea of air-dropping American battalions at strategic points to harass the six North Korean divisions. It was against all prudent military planning to commit small numbers of troops without backup forces, but MacArthur reasoned that the North Korean commanders would conclude that a full-scale attack was on the way and slow down their own invasion.

The bluff worked. Although the American forces were outnumbered a hundred to one, they were able to slow down the advance of the North Korean forces, buying time for the United Nations to take action. The UN Security Council, with the Soviet Union's representative absent, condemned the North Koreans as aggressors and called on all UN members to supply whatever help the South Koreans required to fight the armed attack. According to author John Devaney:

> This was the birth of the United Nations Army in Korea. Commanded by MacArthur, most of its troops were Americans or South Koreans, but there were sprinklings of soldiers from Great Britain, New Zealand, Australia, and other nations. Truman called his sending of American troops a part of "a police action by the United Nations" to "render assistance" to South Korea. It was not the Korean War but the "Korean conflict," the U.S. itself never declaring war on North Korea.[53]

MacArthur was once again in command of an army, but this one was no match for the numerically superior foe.

Dispute over Help from Chiang Kai-shek

An offer of an additional thirty thousand troops came from an unexpected but unacceptable source. Chiang Kai-shek had lost his bid for power in mainland China and was now occupying the island of Formosa. He was offering his help in ex-

Wanting the United States to back him in his struggle for control of China, Chiang Kai-shek offered MacArthur the use of thirty thousand troops.

change for backing by the United States for a planned return to the mainland. Truman wanted no part in the bitter battle over who would rule China. Without permission from his superiors, MacArthur flew to Formosa to discuss Chiang's offer. Truman was outraged that MacArthur would take it upon himself to disobey orders. In Truman's view, MacArthur was risking plunging the United States into an all-out war with China.

New, Yet Old Tactics

Back at his own headquarters, MacArthur conferred with his staff and proposed a daring plan to use what troops they had available to defeat the North Koreans. He would use the trick of "hit them where they ain't." His plan involved an amphibious landing at Inchon on the west coast of Korea, thirty miles north of the capital, Seoul.

There was little support for this idea from his staff. The point of attack was impossibly difficult. Inchon harbor has thirty-foot tides in September; just a few hours after high tide, the water withdraws, leaving two miles of mudflats where invading troops might be pinned down and then annihilated by defenders. Another staff member pointed out that because of the high tides, Inchon was protected with a nine-foot seawall instead of beaches. Where the troops for such an invasion would come from was another problem. MacArthur planned to send the last of the occupation forces from Japan.

MacArthur listened to the discussion and then announced calmly, "On September 15th, gentlemen, we will do the impossi-

ble." [54] He was sure that if his own men thought the action was impossible, so would the enemy.

Inchon

Just before daylight on September 15, 1950, four cruisers and four destroyers steamed up the west coast of Korea. Entering Inchon harbor, they headed for shore to destroy mines and to draw fire from hidden enemy shore batteries. The North Koreans took the bait and opened fire, which pinpointed the location of their gun emplacements for the heavier guns of the UN cruisers. Bombers from four aircraft carriers that had remained beyond the horizon came in next, destroying remaining enemy installations. This was just the prelude to the main assault, however.

MacArthur watched the invasion itself with field glasses from the bridge of the USS *Mt. McKinley*. The first wave of marines took a small island two miles offshore, securing a causeway connecting the island to the mainland. Nothing more could be done until the high tide returned again, twelve hours later. Everything depended on what the North Koreans could rush to Inchon before six o'clock that night.

At high tide, the marines shoved off from the captured island aboard a swarm of landing craft that skimmed up and over the nine-foot seawall. The attackers encountered only light resistance and headed toward Seoul. Here the defense was stronger.

On September 18, the 7th Division, direct from Tokyo, landed at Inchon, outflanking the North Korean army from the south and rear. The city surrendered ten days later. All the land the North Koreans

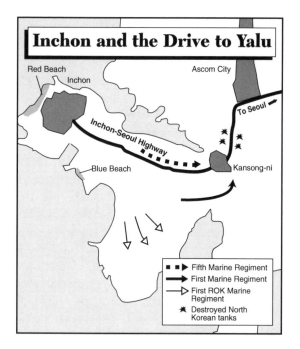

Inchon and the Drive to Yalu

Red Beach
Inchon
Ascom City

To Seoul

Inchon-Seoul Highway

Blue Beach

Kansong-ni

■ ■ ▶ Fifth Marine Regiment
→ First Marine Regiment
▷ First ROK Marine Regiment
✳ Destroyed North Korean tanks

had taken below the 38th parallel was now back in the hands of UN forces. MacArthur was forced to halt his troops while the UN debated whether further force should be used against the North Koreans. A go-ahead was finally granted. MacArthur assured Truman that American troops would be home for Christmas.

An Order to Retreat

American forces did not head home for Christmas after all. The farther north they pushed the more fresh enemy troops they faced. Huge numbers of Chinese "volunteers" were crossing the Yalu River to bolster the North Korean forces. Counterattacks by the northern army were now killing large numbers of UN troops. Raids by Russian planes taking off from bases in Manchuria brought more destruction. Mac-

Arthur ordered the bridges over the Yalu River to be destroyed. Immediately those orders were countermanded by Truman, who hoped to keep China from entering the Korean conflict in full force. To appease China's Mao Tse-tung, Truman had promised that Manchuria's borders would not be violated by UN troops.

In response to the actions of Mac-Arthur, almost a quarter-million Chinese troops surged into North Korea, forcing UN troops to retreat. The attack almost trapped four UN divisions before they could be evacuated by sea. All other UN forces were swept back to the original line south of the 38th parallel, where they dug in for a last-stand defense.

Newspapers that two months before had proclaimed MacArthur a hero for the victory at Inchon now ran stories indicating that he had walked into a well-laid trap. MacArthur tried to explain what had happened, but was ordered by Truman not to give interviews unless they had been cleared by the Department of Defense. Mac-Arthur refused to accept this order.

During the bitter cold of January 1951, North Korean and UN troops clashed repeatedly over the same territory. Meanwhile MacArthur begged Truman in vain for permission to bomb airfields in Manchuria and to use troops from Formosa to back up his own depleted forces. Mac-Arthur angrily contended that the men's lives were being lost in vain. He argued openly in the press and to representatives in Congress that once he had been sent into battle he must be allowed to win. A nation unwilling to make that total military commitment, he said, should not fight at all.

Truman was convinced that MacArthur's plan would bring the United States into a

Containing Communism

MacArthur felt strongly that the outcome of the conflict in Korea would have a lasting effect on the spread of communism throughout the world. In Reminiscences *he defines this philosophy.*

"Seizure of Inchon and Seoul will cut the enemy's supply line and seal off the entire southern peninsula. The vulnerability of the enemy is his supply position. Every step southward extends his transport lines and renders them more frail to dislocation. . . .

The only alternative to a stroke such as I propose will be the continuation of the savage sacrifice we are making at Pusan, with no hope of relief in sight. Are you content to let our troops stay in that bloody perimeter like beef cattle in the slaughterhouse? Who will take the responsibility for such a tragedy? Certainly I will not.

The prestige of the Western world hangs in the balance. Oriental millions are watching the outcome. It is plainly apparent that here in Asia is where the Communist conspirators have elected to make their play for global conquest."

MacArthur and his men move up for the push against the North Korean forces.

devastating war with China. His answer was that this was "the wrong war at the wrong place at the wrong time with the wrong enemy. . . . What would suit the ambitions of the Kremlin better than for our military forces to be committed to a full scale war with China?"[55]

The Recall

The rancor between two strong men, each sure that his view was right, was bound to come to a climax. On April 11, 1951, Truman issued a public statement:

In April 1951, President Truman relieved General MacArthur of his duties and appointed Lieutenant General Matthew Ridgeway (back left).

With deep regret I have concluded that General of the Army Douglas MacArthur is unable to give his whole-hearted support to policies of the United States Government and of the United Nations. . . . I have, therefore, relieved General MacArthur of his command and have designated Lt. General Matthew B. Ridgeway as his successor. . . . General MacArthur's place in history as one of the greatest commanders is fully established. The nation owes him a debt of gratitude for the distinguished and exceptional service which he has rendered his country. . . . I repeat my regret at the necessity for the action I feel compelled to take.[56]

MacArthur was attending an official luncheon when the news of Truman's action was broadcast over the radio. An aide-de-camp heard the announcement and hastened to call the embassy. He first asked to speak to Jean MacArthur. It was she who relayed the news to her husband. His only words were, "Well Jeannie, I guess we're going home."[57]

9 Heading for Home

At daybreak on April 16, 1951, MacArthur's motorcade left the American embassy in Tokyo. Almost a quarter-million Japanese people, waving small Japanese and American flags, lined the twelve miles of highway to the airport. It was an amazing tribute to a general who had defeated Japan in war but rebuilt it in peace.

At the airport cannons boomed a salute while eighteen jet fighters and four superfortresses flew overhead. MacArthur said his farewells to the Japanese leaders and the diplomatic corps. Then he boarded the official plane *Bataan*. The pilot circled the peak of Mount Fuji once and then they were on their way.

MacArthur had been away from home for sixteen years, since he had married Jean. His son had never seen his native country. Momentous changes had taken place, changes that would directly affect MacArthur's future.

When the plane landed in Honolulu, crowds greeted him with cheers. The general was visibly moved by this show of public support. That was only the beginning.

Korean children express support for the United States.

Half a million people gathered outside the St. Francis Hotel to welcome the general home after a sixteen-year absence.

The next stop on their journey was San Francisco. The MacArthurs were treated to a parade strewn with confetti and ticker tape. The last leg of the trip took them to Washington, D.C., where the general had been invited to address a joint session of Congress.

On the afternoon of April 19, 1951, he was escorted to the House chamber of the Capitol. Members of the House of Representatives and Senate had already taken their seats. The general strode to the platform, head held high, this time without the medals and ribbons he was privileged to wear, his only decorations the five stars on each side of his collar. His voice was clear and solemn. MacArthur spoke without bitterness, but in his address stated his firm conviction that Russia must be stopped from spreading its influence in the world. He emphasized that appeasement of aggressors only encourages them. His closing lines were particularly memorable:

I am closing my fifty-two years of military service. When I joined the Army even before the turn of the century, it was the fulfillment of all my boyish hopes and dreams. The world has turned over many times since I took the oath on the Plain at West Point, and the hopes and dreams have long since vanished. But I remember the refrain of one of the most popular barrack ballads of that day which proclaimed most proudly that "Old soldiers never die, they just fade away." And like the old soldier of that ballad, I now close my military career and just fade away—an old soldier who tried to do his duty as God gave him the light to see that duty. Good-bye.[58]

Investigating Committee

Now it was Truman's turn to receive criticism. Many members of Congress reacted negatively to MacArthur's being relieved of his command. On April 25, the Senate unanimously approved a resolution providing for its Armed Services and Foreign Relations Committees to conduct an inquiry into the military situation in the Far East.

MacArthur was called as the first witness. In testimony lasting three days, he admitted no mistakes in the strategic planning of the Korean War. Instead, MacArthur shifted blame to others. He asserted that with adequate intelligence reports about China's buildup of military troops at the border, he would have been warned of impending danger. He insisted that had he been allowed to attack the Yalu River bridges, which gave the enemy direct access to the front, his troops would not have had to retreat from North Korea.

MacArthur's opponents responded by suggesting that with all his knowledge of

When the Senate conducted an inquiry into the military situation in the Far East, MacArthur was called as the first witness.

the Far East, he should have been well informed about China's intentions. No direct conclusions were issued by the congressional committees.

Another Go at Politics

Although MacArthur seemed to have more supporters overseas than at home, he was not ready to fade away just yet. Despite his dramatic farewell before Congress, MacArthur continued to wear his uniform while touring the country and denouncing the Truman administration's policies during the Korean War. Most of his travel expenses, including the use of private planes, were covered by ultraconservative, wealthy Republicans. He criticized Truman's handling of domestic and foreign affairs as well, railing in particular against unjustly high taxes.

Many people were sure that MacArthur was planning to run for president again. The fact that he had failed to win a public vote of confidence in 1948, however, made

Anti-Truman Rhetoric

MacArthur's political speeches made plain his opposition to virtually all of Truman's policies. William Manchester notes one example in American Caesar.

"On Saturday, March 22, 1952, MacArthur capped his campaign against the administration. Standing on the steps of the capitol in Jackson, Mississippi, he charged that administration policies were 'leading toward a Communist state with as dreadful certainty as though the leaders of the Kremlin were charting the course.' He deplored massive American aid to Europe; charity would begin at home, he said, although billions had been spent on the Continent, he doubted that the United States had 'gained a single convert to the cause of freedom or inspired new or deeper friendships' there. Of the Korean truce talks, which had been under way for eight months, he said that 'the only noticeable result is that the enemy had gained time,' and he prophesied that 'our future . . . in Korea will probably mean the ultimate loss of continental Asia.' The *New York Times* protested that 'the bitterness of his attack . . . on the whole of the Marshall Plan, the strengthening of Western Europe, and the rescue of Greece and Turkey does violence to our good name' and was 'a disservice to the public.' So it was, but much of the public— enough of it to swing a close election—didn't think so. . . . MacArthur became a symbol of opposition to the unwinnable war, enthusiasm for which, Acheson's tart phrase, had 'reached an irreducible minimum.' The following Sunday, Truman announced that he would not be a candidate for reelection. MacArthur's nationwide campaign against him had not been the sole reason for the President's decision, but it had been a factor, and MacArthur felt avenged, felt he had achieved one of his goals of that election year."

it hard for key Republicans to take him seriously as a candidate. Richard Nixon later wrote in his memoirs, "In a political sense the last eleven years of MacArthur's life were wasted. His intellectual powers were undiluted, but in the 1950s and early 1960s, because of circumstances, they were not put to use as they should have been."[59]

When MacArthur realized he lacked support for his own candidacy, he turned to trying to defeat Eisenhower's nomination. Following his return from Korea, he openly campaigned on behalf of Senator Robert Taft over Eisenhower for the Republican nomination. Everyone wondered whether there would be verbal fireworks when MacArthur delivered the keynote address at the 1952 Republican National Convention in Chicago. However, his speech did not have the dramatic effect of his "Old soldiers never die" speech before Congress.

He denounced "dangerous reactionaries" of the "war party of American politics and administrative leaders." He aimed his broadsides of crackling rhetoric at "a leadership which by weakness and indecision has brought about such a military dilemma," one that "lacks the soundness of vision, the moral courage and the resolute will to resolve. We must have leadership capable of decision, for indecision in war is but the prelude to disaster." He enumerated the "goals of the Republicans," which included purging the nation's educational system of "subversive and immoral influences." He wanted to "correct social inequities," reduce taxes, stabilize the dollar, and "fortify the initiative and energy of farmers."[60]

Some felt that his ideas wandered from the glory of his country's history to the strength of God's will in determining the future of the nation. His support did little to help Senator Robert Taft.

Some newspaper editorials called him a warmonger, one who delights in war. MacArthur would certainly not have agreed. As he stated in a speech at West Point, the true soldier is never a warmonger, but on the contrary, "prays for peace, for he must suffer and bear the deepest wounds and scars of war."[61]

Yet he was by no means an isolationist. He believed that the United States needed to defend its friends around the world. He also believed that the effects of events in one part of the world would inevitably be felt elsewhere. MacArthur said, "You can't let one-half the world slide into slavery and just confine yourself to defending the other. You have got to hold every place."[62] Although MacArthur found he could not directly influence his government's foreign policy, he refused to fade away.

Final Days

In August 1952, MacArthur accepted a position as chairman of the board of what was then known as the Remington Rand Corporation. More a figurehead than a working executive, his presence lent prestige to the company and he occasionally offered advice on international affairs, opposing, for example, the company's proposed factory in Russia. MacArthur also actively supported increased corporate dealings in Taiwan.

Publishers had offered generous sums of money to MacArthur if he would write his memoirs. In 1960, at the age of eighty, he started on the project. Titled *Reminiscences,* the book was published in 1964.

MacArthur's eightieth birthday party was held at West Point. The academy's

MacArthur at Home

MacArthur was never one to surround himself with ordinary items, and he loved fine furnishings. Geoffrey Perret describes the setting of his final days in Old Soldiers Never Die.

"It was the towers of the Waldorf-Astoria that became MacArthur's last home. The owner, Conrad Hilton, admired MacArthur so much that he knocked three apartments into one to provide the general with a spacious and luxurious dwelling on the thirty-seventh floor. Hilton, it was reported, charged MacArthur a mere $450 a month, which was less than the price of four nights in a Waldorf suite.

The focal point of MacArthur's last home was a huge salon filled with works of Oriental art, many of them gifts from the Japanese. The salon's walls were covered with large paintings with gold frames. There were mementoes from Jean's travels around the Far East. And there was a Japanese butler who greeted guests at the door and ushered them into this room to wait for MacArthur to appear. One old friend who came to call was William Ganoe, MacArthur's adjutant back during his days as superintendent at West Point. 'Alone in the vast splendor, I had the feeling I had barged into a palace,' wrote Ganoe."

choir sang "Happy Birthday." There was a roll call, and every guest was introduced. There were also gifts of sentimental value. Admiral Thomas Kinkaid presented him with the command flag from the *Nashville,* the cruiser that had carried him into the Leyte Gulf. He was also given the chair that he had used while he was army chief of staff. Messages expressing good wishes were read, even one from former President Eisenhower, now that time had dulled the feelings of resentment between the two men.

In July 1961, MacArthur took a final overseas trip to the Philippines for that na-tion's fiftieth independence celebration. It was a sentimental journey. He visited such historic spots as the white beaches of Leyte and the central road through Luzon, now named MacArthur Highway.

On MacArthur's return to the United States, newly elected president John F. Kennedy paid a courtesy call to the general. Being a Democrat and not favoring MacArthur's conservative political ideas, Kennedy planned on staying but a few minutes. Kennedy later said that the talk with MacArthur was one of the most interesting and informative conversations he had ever had. In turn, MacArthur was invited to the White House to continue the conversation; that meeting lasted three hours.

In his last public appearance, MacArthur was invited to West Point to receive the Thayer Award, granted to an American who has performed outstanding service to his or her country. To Jean's gentle pleas that he put his health first and decline the invitation, he responded emphatically, "I will attend the Thayer Award ceremony if I have to crawl on my hands and knees."[63]

On March 6, 1964, he entered the hospital for exploratory surgery. He seemed to rally, but finally his eighty-four-year-old body could take no more. He died on April 5 of acute kidney and liver failure. His wife, Jean, and son, Arthur, were at his bedside.

Last Rites

MacArthur had left detailed instructions for his funeral. Uncharacteristically, he had asked to be buried in a plain GI coffin; his shirt was not to bear his ribbons. His medals were bequeathed to the museum that the city of Norfolk, Virginia, had agreed to build.

The funeral began on the fields of West Point. Twenty-five hundred members of the corps of cadets stood at attention while six cannons roared in salute. In New York City a large group of cadets led a military funeral parade. MacArthur's coffin was then transferred to Washington, D.C., where another formal parade led to the Capitol rotunda. Services were held at Saint Paul's Episcopal Church in Washington. Shigeru Yoshida, head of the Japanese government when MacArthur took command after the surrender, was present; other dignitaries included Lyndon Johnson and Robert Kennedy.

MacArthur's final resting place is Norfolk, Virginia. The crypt lies under the dome of the 114-year-old Norfolk Courthouse, which also houses the relics of his military career. In spite of such awards for

MacArthur's eightieth birthday party was held at West Point. He was given such sentimental gifts as the command flag from the Nashville, the ship that carried him to the shore of Leyte Gulf.

CORREGIDOR ★ NEW GUINEA ★ BORNEO ★

DOUGLAS MACARTHUR
GENERAL OF THE ARMY

MacArthur's final resting place is Norfolk, Virginia's courthouse, where the relics of his military career are on display.

bravery in battle, his statement made five years before his death, "Could I have but a line a century hence crediting a contribution to the advance of peace, I would gladly yield every honor which has been accorded by war,"[64] gives us another view of MacArthur. Each year thousands of tourists visit the site, which includes battle flags, documents, and medals.

MacArthur's widow, now in her nineties, lives quietly in New York City. Their son, Arthur, lives close by.

Notes

Introduction: A Man of Contradictions

1. William Manchester, *American Caesar*. Boston: Little, Brown, 1978, p. 7.

2. Quoted in Manchester, *American Caesar*, p. 4.

3. Quoted in Manchester, *American Caesar*, p. 5.

Chapter 1: The Wild West

4. Quoted in John Devaney, *Douglas MacArthur: Something of a Hero*. New York: G. P. Putnam's Sons, 1979, p. 14.

5. Douglas MacArthur, *Reminiscences*. New York: McGraw-Hill, 1964, p. 15.

6. MacArthur, *Reminiscences*, p. 16.

7. Quoted in Geoffrey Perret, *Old Soldiers Never Die: The Life of Douglas MacArthur*. New York: Random House, 1996, p. 25.

8. Quoted in Norman Finkelstein, *The Emperor General*. New York: Dillon Press, 1989, p. 16.

9. Norman Richards, *People of Destiny: Douglas MacArthur*. Chicago: Childrens Press, 1967, p. 31.

10. Quoted in Richards, *Douglas MacArthur*, p. 32.

Chapter 2: A Young Officer's Training

11. MacArthur, *Reminiscences*, pp. 28–29.

12. Quoted in Richards, *Douglas MacArthur*, p. 39.

13. MacArthur, *Reminiscences*, p. 29.

14. Quoted in Manchester, *American Caesar*, p. 65.

15. Finkelstein, *The Emperor General*, pp. 22–23.

16. MacArthur, *Reminiscences*, p. 30.

17. MacArthur, *Reminiscences*, p. 36.

18. MacArthur, *Reminiscences*, p. 41.

19. MacArthur, *Reminiscences*, pp. 41–42.

Chapter 3: The World at War

20. Quoted in Jules Archer, *Front-Line General: Douglas MacArthur*. New York: Julian Messner, 1963, p. 50.

21. Quoted in Jean Darby, *Douglas MacArthur*. Minneapolis: Lerner, 1989, p. 29.

22. Quoted in Perret, *Old Soldiers Never Die*, p. 105.

23. Quoted in Perret, *Old Soldiers Never Die*, p. 93.

Chapter 4: Back to West Point

24. Quoted in Richards, *Douglas MacArthur*, p. 56.

25. Quoted in Archer, *Front-Line General*, p. 63.

26. Quoted in Archer, *Front-Line General*, p. 63.

27. Quoted in Archer, *Front-Line General*, p. 66.

28. Quoted in D. Clayton James, *The Years of MacArthur*, vol. 1, *1880–1941*. Boston: Houghton Mifflin, 1970, p. 269.

29. Quoted in Army Times Editors, *Banners and the Glory: The Story of Douglas MacArthur*. New York: G. P. Putnam's Sons, 1965, p. 54.

30. James, *The Years of MacArthur*, vol. 1, p. 339.

31. Quoted in Archer, *Front-Line General*, p. 78.

32. Quoted in Archer, *Front-Line General*, p. 81.

33. Quoted in Richards, *Douglas MacArthur*, p. 62.

Chapter 5: World War II

34. Quoted in Army Times Editors, *Banners and the Glory*, p. 94.

35. Quoted in Manchester, *American Caesar*, p. 271.

36. Devaney, *Something of a Hero*, p. 105.

Chapter 6: "I Shall Return"

37. Quoted in Manchester, *American Caesar,* p. 300.

38. Quoted in Darby, *Douglas MacArthur,* pp. 70–71.

39. Quoted in Army Times Editors, *Banners and the Glory,* p. 109.

40. Quoted in Perret, *Old Soldiers Never Die,* p. 403.

41. Quoted in Perret, *Old Soldiers Never Die,* p. 406.

42. Quoted in Richards, *Douglas MacArthur,* p. 74.

43. Quoted in Devaney, *Douglas MacArthur,* p. 126.

44. Quoted in Army Times Editors, *Banners and the Glory,* p. 114.

45. Quoted in Army Times Editors, *Banners and the Glory,* p. 119.

Chapter 7: Surrender

46. Quoted in Richards, *Douglas MacArthur,* p. 78.

47. Quoted in Richards, *Douglas MacArthur,* p. 78.

48. Quoted in Army Times Editors, *Banners and the Glory,* p. 124.

49. Quoted in Manchester, *American Caesar,* p. 466.

50. Quoted in Archer, *Front-Line General,* p. 149.

Chapter 8: Korea

51. Quoted in Archer, *Front-Line General,* p. 157.

52. Quoted in Archer, *Front-Line General,* p. 159.

53. Devaney, *Douglas MacArthur,* p. 61.

54. Quoted in Archer, *Front-Line General,* p. 163.

55. Quoted in Archer, *Front-Line General,* pp. 167–68.

56. Quoted in Archer, *Front-Line General,* p. 169.

57. Quoted in Archer, *Front-Line General,* p. 170.

Chapter 9: Heading for Home

58. Quoted in D. Clayton James, *The Years of MacArthur,* vol. 3, *Triumph & Disaster 1946–1964.* Boston: Houghton Mifflin, 1985, p. 571.

59. Richard Nixon, *Leaders.* New York: Warner Books, 1982, p. 131.

60. Quoted in Army Times Editors, *Banners and the Glory,* pp. 162–63.

61. Quoted in Archer, *Front-Line General,* p. 177.

62. Quoted in James, *The Years of MacArthur,* vol. 3, p. 616.

63. Quoted in Perret, *Old Soldiers Never Die,* p. 584.

64. Quoted in Army Times Editors, *Banners and the Glory,* p. 133.

For Further Reading

Jules Archer, *Front-Line General: Douglas MacArthur.* New York: Julian Messner, 1963. A dramatic account of MacArthur's career, emphasizing the highlights of a controversial life.

Jean Darby, *Douglas MacArthur.* Minneapolis: Lerner, 1989. A condensed and easy-to-read biography of MacArthur that retains all of the important scenes of his career.

John Devaney, *Douglas MacArthur: Something of a Hero.* New York: G. P. Putnam's Sons, 1979. A well-documented but sometimes fictionalized (with unsubstantiated dialogue) biography.

Norman Finkelstein, *The Emperor General.* New York: Dillon Press, 1989. From the Wild West days of MacArthur's youth to his glorious military career and his later entry into politics, Finkelstein tells it all.

Norman Richards, *People of Destiny: Douglas MacArthur.* Chicago: Childrens Press, 1967. A large-size format with excellent pictures and drawings of the dramatic events of MacArthur's life.

Works Consulted

Army Times Editors, *Banners and the Glory: The Story of Douglas MacArthur*. New York: G. P. Putnam's Sons, 1965. The clear text is illustrated with more than a hundred photographs, a number of which were selected from the private MacArthur family album.

John Gunther, *The Riddle of MacArthur*. 1951. Reprint, Boston: Houghton Mifflin, 1985. A personal assessment of a well-known figure by a novelist and historian who interviewed many of his sources.

D. Clayton James, *The Years of MacArthur*. Vol. 1, *1880–1941*. Boston: Houghton Mifflin, 1970. The most detailed book to date on all aspects of MacArthur's earlier career.

——, *The Years of MacArthur*. Vol. 2, *1941–1945*. Boston: Houghton Mifflin, 1975. Covers the important World War II years of MacArthur's military career, giving insights into his personality and his plans for winning the war in the Pacific.

——, *The Years of MacArthur*. Vol. 3, *Triumph & Disaster 1946–1964*. Boston: Houghton Mifflin, 1985. Completing the trilogy, this volume covers all the important events in MacArthur's later life through his death. Details the Korean struggle and his political ambitions. Excellent biographical source.

Douglas MacArthur, *Reminiscences*. New York: McGraw-Hill, 1964. The story of his career as only MacArthur could tell it, dramatically punctuated with intimate portraits of the key personalities of his time.

William Manchester, *American Caesar*. Boston: Little, Brown, 1978. A well-researched biography that challenges the cherished beliefs of MacArthur's fans and critics alike. Includes a useful timeline of important events.

Richard Nixon, *Leaders*. New York: Warner Books, 1982. Nixon knew virtually every foreign leader since World War II. In this book of essays, he covers Douglas MacArthur and Shigeru Yoshida in his chapter "East Meets West"; fascinating insights.

Geoffrey Perret, *Old Soldiers Never Die: The Life of Douglas MacArthur*. New York: Random House, 1996. A biography demythologizing both the praise and criticism heaped on MacArthur during his lifetime.

Richard H. Rovere and Arthur Schlesinger Jr., *The General and the President*. New York: Farrar, Straus, and Young, 1951. A readable, objective appraisal of the events of the Korean War, up to the moment of MacArthur's return to the United States, written by contemporary historians.

Rafael Steinberg and the Editors of Time-Life Books, *Return to the Philippines*. Alexandria, VA: Time-Life Books, 1980. Excellent photographs of the events of MacArthur's struggle to reclaim the Philippines give a stark visual account of war in that arena.

Courtney Whitney, *MacArthur: His Rendezvous with History*. New York: Knopf, 1956. Revealing for its contemporary account of the controversy and divided public opinion surroundin MacArthur.

Index

Picture Credits

Cover photo: Corbis-Bettmann
Sonja Alland/Archive Photos, 38
Archive Photos, 11, 13, 15, 19, 27, 31, 46, 47, 52, 57, 68 (bottom), 74, 77, 86, 87
Archive Photos/American Stock, 32
Corbis-Bettmann, 26
Library of Congress, 43

National Archives, 10, 33, 62, 63, 65, 78, 80
Popperfoto/Archive Photos, 23
© Smithsonian Institute, 64, 66
Scott Swanson/Archive Photos, 50
Harry S. Truman Library, 60
UPI/Corbis-Bettmann, 39, 58, 68 (top), 81, 82

About the Author

Mary Virginia Fox is the author of more than forty books for young readers. As a freelance writer, her work has also appeared in newspapers and magazines. She and her husband lived in the Philippines, Iran, Colombia, South America, and Tunisia for several months at a time, where she continued her writing. She is a graduate of Northwestern University and currently lives in Madison, Wisconsin. She is an instructor for the Institute of Children's Literature.